KWAZULU-NATAL
Heritage Sites

A GUIDE TO SOME GREAT PLACES

KWAZULU-NATAL
Heritage Sites

A GUIDE TO SOME GREAT PLACES

SUE DERWENT

First published in 2006 in southern Africa by David Philip Publishers, an imprint of
New Africa Books (Pty) Ltd, 99 Garfield Road, Claremont 7700, South Africa
(021) 674 4136
www.newafricabooks.co.za

ISBN: 0-86486-653-4

Editing by Jennifer Stastny
Project management and proofreading by Roelien Theron
Layout and design by Fresh Identity
Cover design by Fresh Identity
Printing and binding by Shumani Printers

CONTENTS

AUTHOR'S NOTE

There is as much of a desire in Africa to erase the past as to preserve it: on the one hand, to remove monuments and change street names; on the other, the urge to re-cover, un-cover, dis-cover and honour the history of all of our people. Aside from this, there is pressure in developing countries to modernise and make way for the future. Old buildings may be cleared, trees hundreds of years old chopped down, historic sites allocated for developments and important archaeological sites built over.

The original idea for this book was to showcase the declared national heritage sites that can be found in KwaZulu-Natal: sites that would give an insight into the past. After all, many of the events that took place in KwaZulu-Natal shaped the face of contemporary South Africa. Some of these events and the associated personalities are familiar and even famous, while others, of no less importance or interest, are relatively unknown.

The province is full of fascinating sites of great historic value, many of which are protected and conserved by law. It was difficult to know what to include. With the assistance of Amafa, KwaZulu-Natal's heritage council, I began wading through files of heritage sites. However, owing to apartheid politics and policies, many of the really important sites relating to ethnic and cultural groups other than the European settlers had largely been disregarded and were not yet registered. Hence they would not be found in the files.

So it was back to the drawing board and, with Amafa's assistance, a representative list of historically important, interesting and, sometimes, unconventional heritage 'sites' was drawn up. We included in the list the province's two registered World Heritage Sites: the uKhahlamba-Drakensberg Park, a natural *and* cultural site of international importance, and the Greater St Lucia Wetland Park, a natural heritage site of international significance.

Although many sites were originally deemed unsuitable because they are inaccessible, not open to the public, on private land, or not suitably protected or developed for tourism, we included some anyway, simply because they are fun, interesting or little known. This meant that, at the same time, several other sites had to be omitted because of space constraints.

The final list arrived at for the purposes of this book includes many sites that are already registered heritage sites, as well as many that are earmarked for registration or, thankfully, are in the process of being registered. The selection is by no means conclusive, nor is it an academic documentation of all heritage sites and monuments in the province.

I hope that this book gives you a small taste of the fascinating history of KwaZulu-Natal and of events that helped shape the present. It is intended to help you explore a variety of places across the length and breadth of KwaZulu-Natal and, in the process, to discover the past. I hope that you will enjoy that discovery even more than I did. I found that getting to know a bit more about where we have come from has given me a wonderful sense of belonging, as well as a richer and deeper sense of who South Africans are as a people.

May it do the same for you.

Sue Derwent
Durban

Vasco da Gama Clock, Durban.

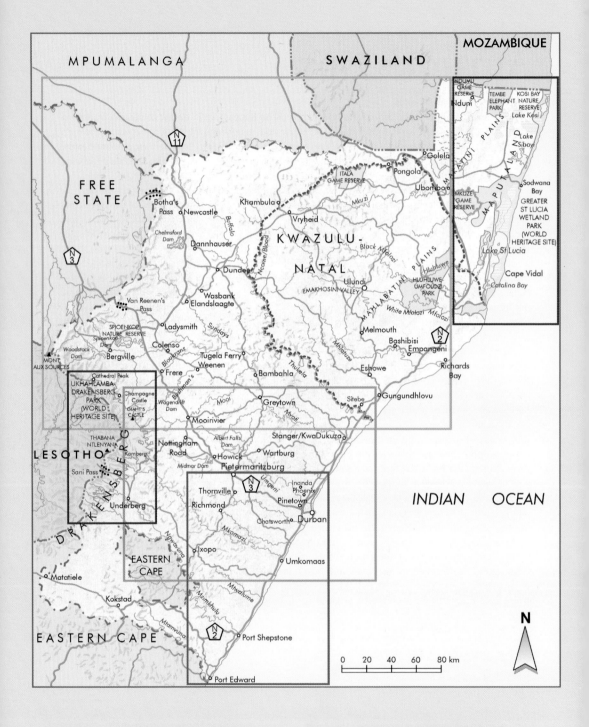

MPUMALANGA

SWAZILAND

MOZAMBIQUE

FREE
STATE

KWAZULU-
NATAL

INDUMU
GAME
RESERVE
Nduni

TEMBE
ELEPHANT
PARK

KOSI BAY
NATURE
RESERVE
Lake Kosi

Lake
Sibayi

Golela

Pongola

ITALA
GAME RESERVE

Ubombo

MKUZE
GAME
RESERVE

Sodwana
Bay
GREATER
ST LUCIA
WETLAND
PARK
(WORLD
HERITAGE
SITE)

Khambula

Vryheid

Mkuzi

Botha's
Pass

Newcastle

Dannhauser

Chelmsford
Dam

Buffalo

Ncome/Blood

Black Mfolozi

MAHLABATINI PLAINS

Hluhluwe

Lake St Lucia

Cape Vidal

N
11

N
3

Dundee

Van Reenen's
Pass

Wasbank
Elandslaagte

Ulundi

EMAKHOSINI VALLEY

HLUHLUWE-
UMFOLOZI
PARK

White Mfolozi

Mfolozi

Catalina Bay

SPIOENKOP
NATURE RESERVE
Spioenkop
Dam

Woodstock
Dam

Ladysmith

Colenso

Sundays

Mhlatuze

Melmouth

Bashibisi
Empangeni

N
2

MONT
AUX SOURCES

Bergville

Blouwkrans

Frere

Tugela Ferry
Weenen

Thukela

Eshowe

Richards
Bay

Cathedral Peak

UKHAHLAMBA-
DRAKENSBERG
PARK
(WORLD
HERITAGE SITE)

Champagne
Castle

GIANT'S
CASTLE

Wagendrift
Dam

Bambahla

Gungundhlovu

Bushman's

Mooi

Greytown

Mvoti

Sitebe

LESOTHO

DRAKENSBERG

THABANA
NTLENYANA

Kamberg

Sani Pass

Mooirivier

Nottingham
Road

Albert Falls
Dam

Howick
Midmar Dam
Pietermaritzburg

Wartburg

Stanger/KwaDukuza

Underberg

Thornville

Richmond

N
3

Umgeni

Inanda
Phoenix

Pinetown

Chatsworth

Durban

INDIAN   OCEAN

EASTERN
CAPE

Ngwangwa

Ixopo

Mkomazi

Umkomaas

Matatiele

Mtwalume

Kokstad

Mzimkhulu

Mtamvuna

N
2

Port Shepstone

EASTERN CAPE

Port Edward

0   20   40   60   80 km

N

Northern and Central KZN

Pietermaritzburg and Midlands

KZN South

Drakensberg and Maputaland

LIST OF MAPS

The maps that are placed in the first three chapters of this book give the location of the main sites. The places that are described in the last chapter (KZN's World Heritage Sites) appear on the map on this page and on the map in the first chapter (Northern and Central KZN).

KEY TO ALL MAPS

—·—·· International boundary

— · — · Provincial boundary

- - - - - - - - Historical Zululand boundary

:::: Pass

○ City

° Town

——— National Road

——— Main road

▢ Buildings, plaques, monuments, grave sites and other areas of interest

⋈ Battle site

⛵ Shipwreck

⚑ Lighthouse

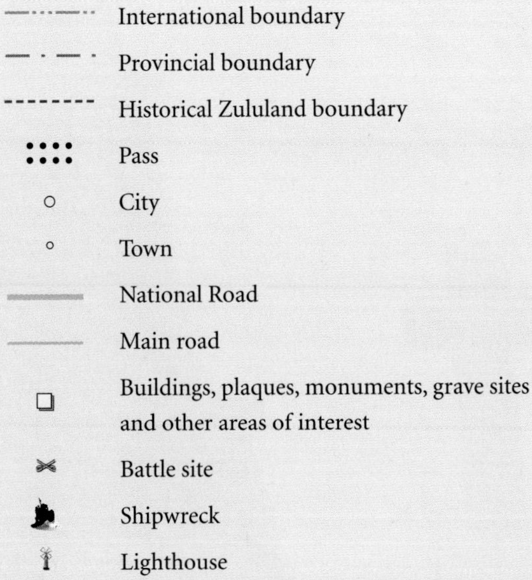

Northern and Central KZN

Over the ages, Stone Age and Iron Age peoples, Bushmen, Nguni pastoralists, and Boer and British settlers have made their home in northern and central KwaZulu-Natal. This part of the country is still largely rural, with sizeable stretches of farmland and small towns. It encompasses the historical kingdom of Zululand – roughly the area to the north of the Thukela River – which ceased to exist in 1897, when it was formally incorporated by the British into Natal.

The Zulu were under the leadership of Shaka's half-brother Dingane, when the first Boers – members of the so-called Kommissie Trek – arrived in Port Natal (Durban) to investigate the possibilities of settlement. Three years later, in 1837, Piet Retief and his party of Voortrekkers crossed the Drakensberg mountains into Natal. There followed a series of battles between Boer and Zulu that ended with the Zulu defeat in 1838 after one of the best known battles in the country's history, the Battle of Ncome/Blood River.

White settlers had been established at Port Natal since 1824 and had travelled into the interior both as missionaries and to trade with the tribes there. In 1843, in response to the establishment of the Boer republic of Natalia, including Port Natal, the British annexed Natal. Despite the defeat of the Zulu by the Boers, the British colonial authorities in Natal continued to view the Zulu kingdom as a threat. Under the instigation of Sir Henry Bartle Frere, they engineered a war with the Zulu, succeeding eventually in breaking up and destroying the kingdom.

Crosses at the Clouston Garden of Remembrance in the vicinity of Colenso are a reminder of the many battles in KwaZulu-Natal's history.

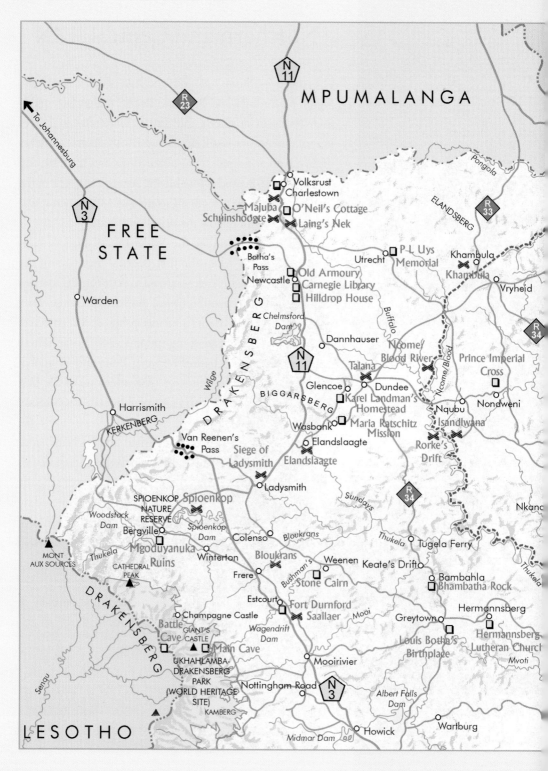

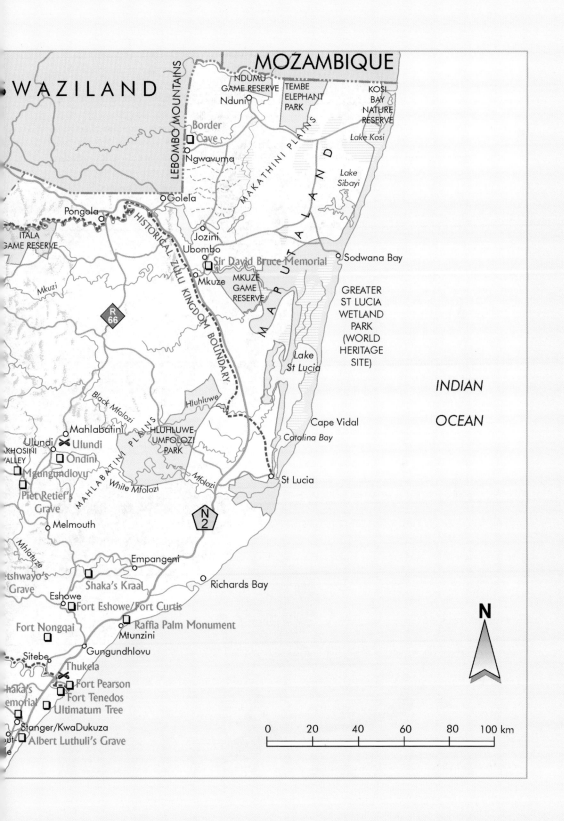

Land of the Zulu

By the late 18th century, the Zulu were just another small and fairly insignificant tribe of Nguni descent. Zulu oral tradition tells of how Malandela, who has been characterised as the father of the Zulu people, settled in the late 16th century on the banks of the Umhlatuze River. The Zulu people are said to have taken their name from one of his sons – Zulu, meaning 'people of the skies' or 'people of the heaven'.

The Zulu were vassals of the powerful Mthetwa clan who, under their leader Dingiswayo, had conquered and absorbed many of the smaller clans in an effort to control access to trade routes as well as to secure scarce natural resources such as grazing. By the early 1800s, however, they had begun to emerge as a distinct regional power under Senzangakhona and, from 1816, his illegitimate son Shaka. As head of the Zulu, Shaka succeeded in defeating the Qwabe in the south and driving the powerful Ndwandwe under their leader Zwide further north. Zulu dominance was established under Shaka in the region between the Mfolozi River to the north and the Thukela River to the south.

In and around eMakhosini

eMakhosini (literally 'the valley of the chiefs') lies southwest of Ulundi. Surrounding the valley are several stone-walled structures associated with the powerful Buthelezi and Khumalo Bantu-speaking clans. These clans later played a significant role in the formation of the Zulu kingdom. The famous king, Shaka Zulu, was born in this valley around 1785, and it is here that his forebears, Nkosinkulu Zulu, Phunga, Mageba, Ndaba, Jama and Senzangakhona, lie buried.

The graves and royal residences of four Zulu rulers – Shaka, Dingane, Mpande and Cetshwayo, who ruled in succession from 1816 to 1884 – are located in the area around eMakhosini. The royal residences of Zulu kings Dingane and Cetshwayo have been partially reconstructed and Cetshwayo's royal residence, Ondini, today includes a small but fascinating site museum and the KwaZulu Cultural Museum.

Other interesting sites in and around eMakhosini have recently been opened to the public. An old farmhouse adjacent to kwaGqokli hill, where King Shaka achieved his first military success against the powerful Ndwandwe under *inkosi*

A symbolic traditional Zulu beer pot on a beaded ring marks the entrance to the eMakhosini valley. It is surrounded by sculptured horns and tusks of indigenous animals once found in this area.

Mgoduyanuka ruins

This archaeological site dates back to the Iron Age and bears some unique features, including several middens. Radiocarbon dating shows that Mgoduyanuka was also occupied in the 17th and 18th centuries. Oral history suggests that the settlements were built by the amaZizi people who lived in the Bergville district until the period of Shaka's expansion in the 1820s.

One settlement in this site consists of a number of circular and oval enclosures at the base of Mgoduyanuka hill, overlooking the Thukela River near Bergville. Some of the enclosures are thought to have been livestock pens and were surrounded by a ring of huts, of which now only the floors remain. Another settlement had an unusual, sinuous passage-entrance to its animal enclosure, while a third had a line of enclosures surrounded by a ring of huts. The site appears to have been occupied for several decades, and there is evidence of four phases of construction.

Zwide of the Ndwandwe, has been converted into a luxury lodge. The secretary to Field Marshal Jan Christiaan Smuts once occupied this lovely Victorian homestead.

eMakhosini also bears testimony to the Voortrekkers. Voortrekker leader Piet Retief lies buried in the valley at kwaMatiwane, the Hill of Execution. There is a monument to him and his fallen comrades not far from the partially recon-structed isiGodlo, or royal enclosure, of Mgun-gundlovu, King Dingane's royal residence. The grave of Dirkie Uys, another famous Voortrekker, has recently been discovered in the area.

Visit the graves

Traditionally, each Zulu king built his own homestead and was buried near it when he died. The graves of Nkosinkulu Zulu (c. 1627–1709), Phunga (c. 1657–1727), Ndaba (c. 1697–1763), and Jama (c. 1727–1781), the father of Senzangakhona (c. 1757–1816), are all situated in the eMakhosini valley, as is the grave of Mageba (c. 1660–1745), which lies close to the Umzinhlanga stream in eMakhosini.

The graves of the chiefs and kings are not easy to find. For assistance call Amafa/ Heritage KwaZulu-Natal (035 870 2050/12) at Ondini, just outside Ulundi.

Nobamba and Siklibheni

Nobamba and Siklibheni are the two most hallowed sites in eMakhosini.

It was at Siklibheni that the original *nkatha ka Zulu* was made. The *nkatha ka Zulu* is the royal roll or royal ring, a sacred object of royal regalia made from special grasses and herbal plants and covered with the skin of a python.

Siklibheni was the residence of *inkosi* Senzanga-khona ka Jama Zulu, (c. 1757–1816), father of Shaka, Dingane and Mpande – three successive kings – and grandfather of Cetshwayo. King Shaka and other chiefs would make a pilgrimage to this homestead before an important military excursion. A stone cairn marks Senzangakhona's grave and the site of the royal residence. Senzangakhona's monument is about ten kilometres from kwaGqokli hill where Shaka scored his victory over Zwide.

Not far away is the burial site of Mthaniya, mother of Senzangakhona. And over the hills is Nobamba, where the homesteads of Kings Jama and Dinuzulu once stood. Dinuzulu, the son of Cetshwayo, reigned from 1884 to 1888 and again from 1898 to 1907. He is buried at Nobamba beneath a granite slab at the site of Senzangakhona's birthplace (at the foot of the Ntabaye Zulu hill).

When Cetshwayo was captured and sent to Cape Town, he asked one of his counsellors, Zibebhu, to take care of the young Dinuzulu. This responsibility later fell on Cetshwayo's brother, Ndabuko. After Cetshwayo's reinstatement, Zibebhu betrayed the king, and attacked and defeated Ndabuko. Cetshwayo launched a return attack, but was injured and fled to Nkandla. After Cetshwayo's death in 1884, Dinuzulu defeated Zibebhu with the help of a Boer commando.

Dinuzulu was eventually captured by the Brit-ish, convicted on a charge of high treason and sent to St Helena Island. He was allowed to return in 1898, but was again convicted in 1907 after being implicated in the Bhambatha uprising. He was again deported, this time to the former Transvaal.

kwaDukuza: Shaka's last residence

kwaDukuza was the last of the royal residences of the legendary warrior and king, Shaka (c. 1787–1828).

Shaka was the illegitimate son of Senzangakhona by Nandi of the Langeni tribe. He was constantly subjected to derision for his illegitimate status. Shaka and his mother were banished by Senzangakhona when Shaka was around six years of age. The two outcasts eventually found a home in the homestead of the Mthethwa clan under Dingiswayo. As Shaka matured, his reputation grew, and he attracted the attention of Dingiswayo, who had by now built up a federation of more than 50 tribes through warfare and diplomacy. Shaka became a leading warrior in Dingiswayo's army, refining fighting tactics and weaponry and further earning the king's respect. With Dingiswayo's support, Shaka took the Zulu throne in 1816.

In April 1818, Shaka met the forces of the powerful chief Zwide of the Ndwandwe tribe at kwaGqokli hill. He enjoyed a tactical victory, followed by another at kwaBulawayo, his first homestead, located in the eMakhosini valley. His victory over Zwide cost him 1 500 warriors. On his side, Zwide lost some 7 500 men, including four of his sons.

In 1828, Shaka's half-brothers, Dingane and Mhlangana, fearing for their lives and resentful at being denied the Zulu throne, had Shaka killed, with the help of his *induna*, Mbopa. Shaka was stabbed to death on 22 September of that year at kwaDukuza.

Mgungundlovu: Dingane's capital

Mgungundlovu was the royal capital of Zululand during the reign of Shaka's half-brother, Dingane (c. 1795–1840). Roughly translated, Mgungundlovu means 'the secret place of the elephant', *ndlovu* meaning elephant, a traditional reference to the stature of the king. When the Boers advanced in 1838 to exact revenge for Zulu attacks on Bloukrans and Weenen, King Dingane fled Mgungundlovu after ordering that it be burnt down.

In recent years, parts of the massive royal enclosure and military barracks, which housed approximately 7 000 people, have been reconstructed. Archaeological excavations have uncovered the charcoal remains of the enclosure's outer palisade, as well as a copper-smithing site and grain pits. The excavations further revealed many of the dwelling's original mud-and-dung floors, which had been baked hard by the fire. One of the uncovered floors had a diameter of about ten metres and was surrounded by the charred ruins of 22 structural posts. The sheer size of the structure – thought to be the biggest built in traditional Zulu style – as well as the remains of a unique flower-shaped hearth (much like the one often mentioned by visitors to Mgungundlovu) indicate that this was, indeed, the king's residence.

Near to the entrance of Mgungundlovu is the grave of Nkosinkhulu kaMalandela (1627–1709), who is considered to be the progenitor of the Zulu people and founder of the Zulu royal dynasty. It is thought that Malandela's homestead was situated nearby, close to the Mkhumbane stream.

About five kilometres away from Mgungundlovu is the Mthonjaneni spring, believed to have been the place where King Dingane's wives drew water for his personal use.

Visit sites from Shaka's life

The exact spot of Shaka's death is thought to be where an old mahogany tree now grows in the grounds of the Stanger/ KwaDukuza municipal offices. The grain pit where Dingane is thought to have secretly buried him is marked by a large rock in the **King Shaka Memorial Garden** in the town. The Zulu people erected this memorial during the reign of King Solomon (1913–1932). An interpretative centre has since been added.

Also in the town near King Shaka's memorial, is a small river known as **Shaka's Spring**. From here, unpolluted water was collected for the king's use. Nearby, on the Imbozamo River, was **Shaka's Bathing Pool** and **Shaka's Cave** where he would rest after swimming. Not much further off is the infamous **Execution Cliff** where executions were carried out on Shaka's orders.

Displays at the museum at Nodwengu depict Zulu life during the reign of King Mpande.

The remains of the second Ondini can be found about five kilometres south of Ulundi. The site has been little disturbed since its destruction more than a hundred years ago, although the royal enclosure has been partially reconstructed. Many of the hearths and mud floors – including the floor of Cetshwayo's great hut, which measured approximately 8.5 metres in diameter – have also been restored. There is a museum nearby, with an interpretative centre and a statue of Cetshwayo.

Nodwengu: Mpande's capital

Nodwengu on the Mahlabatini plains (now part of Ulundi) was the Zulu capital during the reign of King Mpande, father of Cetshwayo and half-brother of Shaka and Dingane. Mpande reigned for 32 years and helped to steer the Zulu kingdom through a time of rapid and far-reaching political change. During his reign the Zulu nation enjoyed a relatively peaceful period in its history. Mpande died a natural death in late 1872 and was buried at Nodwengu. A site museum has been erected in Ulundi, next to the grave.

Cetshwayo's three Ondinis

Ondini, which means 'high place' in Zulu, was the military capital of King Cetshwayo (1826–1884). There were actually three Ondinis, the second being Cetshwayo's military capital before he was sent into exile.

The first Ondini was Cetshwayo's homestead before he succeeded his father, Mpande. Cetshwayo destroyed the royal residence after his father's death, as decreed by Zulu custom, and built the second Ondini in the vicinity of the Mahlabatini plains. It covered 60 hectares and was modelled on the great residence of King Dingane at Mgungundlovu. This Ondini was largely destroyed when the British set fire to it after the Battle of Ulundi in 1879. Cetshwayo was exiled but later reinstated as Paramount Chief. He returned to his kingdom and built the third Ondini, south of the former one. By then, however, the Zulu leadership was divided. Civil war followed Cetshwayo's reinstatement and he himself was driven from Ondini in 1883.

Cetshwayo's statue surveys the scene of the king's former residence, Ondini.

Luck of the *isivivane*

It is a common practice among Zulu people, especially in the rural areas, to place piles of stones on a journey. These *isivivane*, or good luck cairns, are scattered throughout southern Africa, especially alongside old, well-used footpaths. *Isivivane* also mark the graves of important people from, or the sites of, homesteads that have been moved.

For example, a traveller will deposit a special stone at the place from which he heads out. A military leader will do the same before setting off on a campaign. To begin an *isivivane*, one should pick up a stone with the toes of the left foot, take it up in the right hand, spit on it and place it on a spot. Once a stone has been placed, custom requires that everyone passing should add a stone to the pile. This is thought to ensure good luck.

The cairn that is found ten kilometres from Weenen on the Muden road is one of the largest and best known in the region. Nowadays, local Zulus refer to the area as eSivivaneni, which means 'the place of the *isivivane*'. The origin of this *isivivane* is not known.

Prince Dabulamanzi kaMpande's grave

It is thought that Prince Dabulamanzi ka-Mpande, an important military commander in the Zulu army and a member of the Zulu royal house during Cetshwayo's rule, is buried at Nondweni. The prince commanded the Undi corps and the uThulwana, inDluyengwe, inDlondlo and uDloko regiments. He led the reserve force that attacked Lord Frederick Chelmsford's depot at Rorke's Drift.

Prince Dabulamanzi openly opposed the division of Zululand by the British into 13 territories after the Zulu defeat at the Battle of Ulundi on 3 July 1879. He also opposed Boer claims to territory in return for their assistance at the Battle of Tshaneni in 1884. With relations tense all round, it was eventually Boer hostility that led to Dabulamanzi's murder at Nondweni in 1886 at the hands of a man named Paul van der Berg.

There is some controversy about the site of Dabulamanzi's grave. Nondweni is one of two possibilities, the other being Stewart Farm at Eshowe. However, since the grave at this site is also claimed by the Shange people as that of their ancestor, *inkosi* Shange, it is more likely that Dabulamanzi is buried at Nondweni in a grave marked by a traditional cairn of stones.

Monuments such as this one to Piet Retief and his comrades are scattered throughout the region.

Piet Retief's grave

After descending into Natal in 1837, Piet Retief wrote a letter to King Dingane stating that he wanted to live in peace with the Zulu nation. In the same letter Retief pointedly highlighted the Voortrekker victory over King Mzilikazi of the Ndebele. Dingane responded by saying that he would concede land to the Voortrekkers if Retief retrieved stolen cattle from Chief Sekonyela of the Batlokwa, apparently as a test of the Voortrekkers' military strength.

Retief's success in the task was enough to convince Dingane that the Zulu would stand no chance against the Voortrekkers in open battle.

Voortrekker leader Piet Retief lies buried at the foot of kwaMatiwane, the Hill of Execution.

This, together with the veiled threat in the letter, was sufficient motivation for Dingane to plot Retief's death. He invited Retief to Mgungundlovu, his royal residence, on 6 February 1838 to sign the land concession. Afterwards, Dingane invited the Boers to lay down their arms and celebrate. During the dancing, the king ordered his soldiers to kill Retief and his party. They were dragged to kwaMatiwane, the Hill of Execution, where they were clubbed to death. Dingane then sent his *impi* out to attack the Voortrekkers' laagers.

The bodies of Retief and his men remained on kwaMatiwane until the Voortrekkers found them later in the year after they had attacked the Zulu royal homestead from which Dingane had already fled. They were buried at the foot of the mountain and a monument was erected in their memory in 1922.

Land of battle

In the 1800s and 1900s, northern and central KwaZulu-Natal echoed with the sound of the battles that were fought between Zulu, Boer and British. The British lost many soldiers in the region before defeating the Zulu in the Anglo-Zulu War of 1879 and the Boers in the first and second Anglo-Boer wars. During these dangerous times they established a number of forts. One such, Fort Nolela, was not far from the White Mfolozi River, where the British forces under Lord Chelmsford camped in July 1879 before crossing the river to engage the Zulu army in the final battle of the Anglo-Zulu War at Ulundi.

The South Africa of today has emerged from these and other conflicts. Graves, monuments, stone cairns, statues and the names of the sites themselves are our legacy.

Giants of Zululand

The Zululand coast, near the site of Shaka's kraal, is one of the few areas in the country where you can still see massive stands of raffia palms, some of which are up to 25 metres tall. The only other place they are found is in the far north, around Kosi Bay on the Mozambique border.

The Raffia Palm Monument is found in Mtunzini, which means 'place of shade' in Zulu. A wooden boardwalk and paths meander through the palms around the village. Interestingly, the palms at Mtunzini were planted and are not a natural occurrence. The rare Palm Nut Vulture, which feeds on the nuts of the raffia palms, is an occasional visitor.

Voortrekker laagers
A laager is a defensive strategy in which wagons are strapped end to end in a large circle with cattle and other valuable property safely tucked inside. In this way the Voortrekkers, who were crossing the Drakensberg mountains into Natal, hoped to be able to safeguard themselves from attack on all sides.

After he had executed Piet Retief and his party in February 1838, King Dingane sent his *impi* out to attack the Voortrekker laagers. Rensburgkoppie (under the leadership of Van Rensburg), Doornkop (Piet Retief's laager), Veglaer and Saailaer (both positioned near Loskop) and Modderlaer (a combination of the remains of Retief's and Piet Uys's laagers) were all attacked during that fateful year. The bloodiest attack took place on the night of 16 February 1838, later to be known as the Night of the Great Murder.

Landmarks of Zulu-Boer conflict
Disenchanted with British rule, Boers in the Cape embarked on the Great Trek. Patrols were sent out in July 1837 by Voortrekker leader Piet Retief to find routes over the Drakensberg mountains into Natal. They returned having found five possible routes and, later that same year, 14 Voortrekkers in four ox wagons made the first crossing. The pass they used (declared a national monument in February 1977) became known as Retief's Pass. By the end of the year, 66 wagons had navigated the difficult pass. Other Voortrekker groups soon followed. The pass was in use for about 30 years.

Bloukrans
Despite Piet Retief's warnings, the Voortrekker parties that were crossing into Natal in 1837 soon scattered south of the Thukela River along the Bloukrans and Bushman's rivers. On the night of 16 February 1838 their laagers were attacked by Zulu warriors, and 96 adults, 185 children and about 200 servants were killed by a Zulu force that also seized about 25 000 head of cattle.

In the days following the attack the Voortrekkers buried their dead in a mass grave near the Great Moordspruit River. In 1895, the bodies were exhumed and reburied under the Bloukrans monument at the site of the battle.

The bodies of Voortrekkers and their servants who were killed by Zulu warriors on the night of 16 February 1838 lie buried under Bloukrans memorial.

Sixty-four bronze ox wagons mark the site of the battle between the Zulu and Voortrekkers that caused the Ncome River to run red with blood.

Saailaer

Saailaer, also known as Zaaylager, on the outskirts of Estcourt (near Fort Durnford), was the camp of Voortrekker leader Gert Maritz. It was the southernmost of the Voortrekker laagers, Maritz having carefully positioned it in a horseshoe bend on the Bushman's River. Because it was not in their direct line of advance, the Zulu warriors did not attack Saailaer on the night of 16 February 1838. When the attack eventually came, the Saailaer Voortrekkers were prepared: as the *impi* made a human chain to cross the flooded Bushman's River they were systematically shot down. They eventually gave up the attack, and Maritz and a small commando were able to rush to the assistance of the other laagers.

Ncome/Blood River

By November 1838 the Voortrekkers had chosen Andries Pretorius as their new leader in the fight against the *impis* that the Zulu king Dingane had sent to 'eat them up'. In December a scout patrol reported seeing a large Zulu presence nearby. Pretorius promptly ordered his commandos to form a laager between the Ncome River and a deep donga. The only unprotected flank faced an open plain. Pretorius placed cannons at three openings between the securely tied wagons. He and his men made a vow that should God grant them victory, they would honour the day forever.

The spears of the attacking Zulu warriors were no match for muskets and cannons, and the Zulu fell back in hundreds, choking the river with their dead and dying until it ran red with blood. It has been known as Blood River ever since.

Pretorius then attacked Dingane's royal homestead at Mgungundlovu, south of present-day Ulundi. However, Dingane had fled before they arrived, setting his royal residence alight behind him. The Boers arrived to find the massive kraal deserted and in flames.

Sixty-four bronze ox wagons arranged in the precise laager formation used by the Voortrekkers, mark the site of the Battle of Ncome/Blood River, near Dundee. For many years, December 16, the day on which the battle was fought, was known as the Day of the Vow. It is now remembered as the Day of Reconciliation.

Karel Landman's homestead

Karel Landman was a renowned commandant in the Great Trek and served as second in command at the Battle of Ncome/Blood River. He took part in the ill-fated April 1838 expedition to Mgungundlovu led by Pieter Uys and Hendrik Potgieter following the death of Piet Retief and his party.

When he first moved to Natal, Landman and his party lived in the so-called Laager of Poles at the mouth of the Umgeni River. He acted as the leader of the Voortrekkers in Natal until the arrival of Andries Pretorius.

In 1852, Landman built a homestead – probably with his own hands, as he was a good builder – on the farm Uithoek, south of Glencoe. He lived there until his death in 1875, and his grave is not far from the house. Sadly, the house was damaged by fire in 1966. The walls survived and the house was subsequently restored with building materials similar to those used in the original house: thatch for the roof, yellowwood for frames and dung for the floor.

Historic markers of the Anglo-Zulu War

A year after the defeat of the Zulu army at Ncome/Blood River in December 1838, Dingane was overthrown by his brother Mpande, with the support of the Boers. Mpande ruled until his death in 1872, but the real power in the Zulu kingdom rested in the hands of his son Cetshwayo. As king, Cetshwayo was determined to resist the Boer advance into his territory, initially looking to Britain for support. The arrival in March 1877 of Sir Bartle Frere, the British High Commissioner for South Africa and Commander-in-Chief of all British forces, brought a new threat to Zulu independence. Sir Bartle Frere was committed to the plan of confederating southern Africa under the British sphere of influence and war between the British and the kingdom of Zululand became inevitable.

Isandlwana

Much has been written about two of the most famous battles of the Anglo-Zulu War: Isandlwana and Rorke's Drift.

On 17 January 1879, a Zulu army of about 20 000 warriors under the command of Mavumengwana kaNdlela Ntuli marched from kwaNodwengu to confront the British force camped at the mountain known as Isandlwana.

A massive bronze replica of a traditional Zulu neckpiece honours the Zulu warriors who died at the Battle of Isandlwana.

Ultimatum Tree

On 11 December 1878, four decades after the Battle of Ncome/Blood River, British officials presented the Zulu leadership with an ultimatum that was engineered to facilitate a British invasion and to end the existence of Zululand as an independent kingdom.

Representing the colonial authorities were, among others, Sir Theophilus Shepstone, Charles Brownlee, Henry Francis Fynn and Colonel Forestier Walker. King Cetshwayo was represented by Vumandaba, the white trader and chief John Dunn, and 13 other principal and subordinate chiefs. Under the terms of the ultimatum, Cetshwayo was to disband his army, pay the British a fine of 500 cattle and hand over a Zulu man accused of murder – terms that were impossible to accept. This shameful manoeuvre led to the Anglo-Zulu War of 1879 and the end of the reign of the last independent Zulu king.

The ultimatum that started the war was issued under a sycamore fig tree at Fort Pearson, known as the Ultimatum Tree, on the banks of the Thukela River. The tree itself was all but destroyed in a cyclone in 1987 and has been declared a national monument.

Just after midday on 22 January 1879, the unprepared British – who had not even bothered to construct proper defensive positions around the camp – were taken by surprise when a huge force of *impi* launched a furious attack. By mid-afternoon the camp had been overrun and about 1 357 people on the British side and 3 000 on the Zulu side had died in a furious three-hour battle in which Zulu spears and shields were pitted against the guns of the British, who were 'making every round count'. Only a few from the British camp survived by fleeing on horseback around the back of Mpethe hill and crossing the Mzinyathi (Buffalo) River.

Isandlwana was the worst defeat suffered by a colonial power in Africa.

The foot of the sphinx-like mountain of Isandlwana is scattered with graves and monuments to the British soldiers who died in this major Zulu victory.

St Vincent's Mission

After the Battle of Isandlwana on 22 January 1879 (St Vincent's Day), Bishop William Kenneth Macrorie asked Charles Johnson, a lay catechist who spoke Zulu, to establish a mission on a site overlooking the Isandlwana battlefield. In 1880, Archdeacon Douglas McKenzie, a Cambridge mathematician and former vice-principal of St Andrew's School in both Grahamstown and in Bloemfontein, was designated by the Bishop of Cape Town to serve at St Vincent's Mission at Isandlwana. McKenzie was consecrated Bishop of Zululand on St Andrew's Day, 30 November 1880.

Construction of the church at the mission began in 1882. Masons cut a sandstone block from the Isandlwana mountain and carved it into a Greek cross above the date of the battle. The foundation stone was laid on an 1879 shilling, an artillery button and a badge of the 24th Regiment. By February 1883, the roof was up and the floor was being paved with shale from a nearby stream.

After setting up St Vincent's, Johnson went on to establish a new mission, St Augustine's, ten kilometres away from Isandlwana. Bishop McKenzie remained at St Vincent's Mission until his death in January 1890. There was no coffin for his burial, and his robed body was laid out simply on a yellowwood plank before the altar of the little church. There he remained on view, chalice in hands, until his funeral just before sunset. A fund in his memory was used to build a catechism school known as McKenzie College. This is now a small museum and interpretative centre.

British soldiers (below) in a tableau at Rorke's Drift Museum. Many soldiers received the highest award for bravery, the Victoria Cross, following the battle at Rorke's Drift.

Rorke's Drift

Rorke's Drift, which takes its name from James Rorke, a trader and farmer, was one of the oldest and best-known crossings of the Buffalo River. A small mission and supply depot was established there.

On the same day that the British camp at Isandlwana was attacked, another party of Zulu warriors attacked the small settlement at Rorke's Drift. This time the Zulu were repulsed by 100-odd British soldiers.

Visit Rorke's Drift Museum

A small but comprehensive museum (034 642 1687) is housed in a thatched mission house that was used as a hospital at the time of the battle. Keep an eye out for the self-guided trail, as well as the arts and crafts centre where you can buy locally made ceramics, painted fabrics and woven articles.

Khambula

On the afternoon of 29 March 1879, a Zulu army of about 20 000 warriors under the command of Chief Mnyamana Buthelezi attacked the British under Colonel (later Field Marshal) Sir Evelyn Wood at Khambula in the north of Zululand. The battle lasted nearly four hours, after which the Zulu were forced to withdraw, their casualties numbering 2 000. Many of the Zulu warriors who fell were buried at Khambula. This was a major defeat for the Zulu. Many of the warriors who fought and fell at Khambula had been among the victors at the Battle of Isandlwana two months earlier.

Rorke's Drift is one the country's best-known battlefields.

Grave of Piet Lafras Uys

Piet Uys was the son of the Voortrekker leader of the same name and brother to the young hero, Dirkie Uys. His father and brother were both killed in the 1838 Battle of Ithaleni. Piet Uys volunteered to serve the colonial government at the start of the Anglo-Zulu War of 1879. Together with a number of Dutch burghers, he took part in a raid on the abaQulusi kraal in January 1879. Later, under the leadership of Colonel Redvers Buller, Uys participated in another raid on the abaQulusi, who were encamped on Hlobane mountain. On 28 March 1879, their small force was overwhelmed, but broke through the Zulu lines and escaped down the mountain. Buller earned the Victoria Cross for his efforts. Uys, who had been with him, went back to help his men and was stabbed in the back by a Zulu warrior.

In 1881, Uys's comrades erected a memorial to him at the place where he fell.

Ulundi

The last battle of the Anglo-Zulu War of 1879 took place close to present-day Ulundi.

Determined to deal a death blow to the Zulu kingdom, the British began to close in on Cetshwayo's capital, Ulundi. The British arrived at a position on the banks of the White Umfolozi River overlooking Ulundi late in June 1879. On July 3, a patrol led by Colonel Redvers Buller was sent to reconnoitre the plain in front of Ulundi across the river and very nearly came to grief when ambushed by the Zulu. The following day at daybreak, the main British force, of just over 5 000 men, 2 Gatling guns and 12 artillery pieces, crossed the river.

The British formed a hollow square and began to advance across the plain where 20 000 Zulu warriors awaited them. The mounted troops under Buller engaged the enemy first but retired into the square when the full weight of the Zulu attack was unleashed. The battle lasted less than three-quarters of an hour and, despite the great courage and determination with which they pressed home their attack, few Zulu warriors managed to get within 30 metres of the square. Only 12 men were killed on the British side, while the Zulu are thought to have lost up to 1 500 in the battle that effectively ended the war, the rule of King Cetshwayo and the independence of the Zulu kingdom

White stones, aloes and a small domed memorial that marks the position of the British are among a number of poignant memorials at the Ulundi battlefield site.

The beautiful and unusual monument on the battle site of Ulundi honours those who died during this decisive battle.

16

A French prince in Africa

One of the most unlikely victims of the Anglo-Zulu War was the Prince Imperial, Napoleon Eugene Louis Jean Joseph.

After the fall of the Second French Empire, the Prince Imperial and his family were exiled to England where, in 1872, he became a military cadet. When the Anglo-Zulu War broke out in 1879, the Prince Imperial, keen to gain some military experience, asked to go to South Africa. The British authorities were not happy with this request and at first turned him down, but eventually gave him permission to sail to South Africa in a private capacity as a 'spectator'. He arrived in Durban on 31 March 1879 and was employed as an aide-de-camp to Lord Chelmsford.

On the morning of 1 June 1879, the Prince Imperial and a number of mounted soldiers left camp on a routine misson. The party was ambushed and attacked when they stopped in the afternoon near the Ityotyozi River. Although a fine horseman, the 23-year-old prince was unable to mount his horse, which bolted, trampling him in the process. He tried to face his attackers but was overcome and stabbed 17 times.

After the war, Zulu warriors who had taken part in the attack praised the prince's bravery, saying he had fought like a lion. A stone cross was erected in his memory in 1880 during a visit to South Arica by his mother, Empress Eugénie.

Battle sites of the Anglo-Boer wars

The first Anglo-Boer War (Transvaal War of Independence) was triggered by the British annexation of the Transvaal (Zuid-Afrikaansche Republiek) in 1877. War broke out in 1888. The first phase was played out in the Transvaal, but several battles took place in Natal: Laing's Nek, Schuinshoogte and Majuba.

The first shots in the second phase of the conflict (1899–1902) were fired at Kraaipan, on the southwestern border of the Transvaal Republic. The first real battle in the three-year war took place at Talana, near Dundee, on 20 October 1899, followed the next day by the Battle of Elandslaagte.

Laing's Nek

On 28 January 1881, a British force of 1 200 men under the command of Major-General Sir George Pomeroy Colley left the town of Newcastle and advanced to the Transvaal border to relieve British garrisons there. Before they could get there, however, they were headed off by Boer Commandant-General Piet Joubert and 2 000 of his men, who were positioned at Laing's Nek, just south of Volksrust. The British were repulsed and retired to camp at Mount Prospect, having suffered casualties of 83 dead and 100 wounded.

Schuinshoogte (Ingogo River)

On 7 February 1881, a mail wagon and its escort were ambushed by the Boers. General Colley decided to increase the escort for the mail wagon the following day and to take command himself. Some 300 Boers attacked the convoy at the Ingogo River. The British lost 139 men before retiring.

Majuba

On the night of 26 February 1881, General Colley and about 370 men took the summit of Majuba mountain, from where they started firing down on the Boer camp early the following morning. Colley's men had no artillery or machine guns and they had not made effective entrenchments. It did not take long for Boer volunteers, supported by fire from the foot of the mountain, to scale the mountain and dislodge the British. By afternoon the battle was over. Colley and 91 of his men were killed, 134 men were wounded and 59 taken prisoner. Colley was buried at his camp at Mount Prospect and a monument was later erected at the place where he had fallen. The Boers lost two men.

Talana and Elandslaagte

The first real battle in the second Anglo-Boer War (1899–1902), today known as the South African War, took place at Talana, near Dundee, on 20 October 1899. Boer forces under General Lucas Meyer occupied Talana hill from where they shelled Dundee. The battle was deemed a success for the British under General Penn Symons. At Elandslaagte the following day, the British, under Major-General French, managed to dislodge a force of Boers under General Jan Kock who had occupied Elandslaagte and were intent on cutting the railway line between Lady-smith and Glencoe.

An obelisk at Elandslaagte near the Boer memorial commemorates Lieutenant Colonel Scott-Chrisholme, a prominent British soldier and commander of the Imperial Light Horse brigade. Further along the road is a cemetery with the graves of some of the British soldiers who died at the Battle of Elandslaagte.

Visit Talana Museum

The Talana Museum on the outskirts of Dundee (034 212 2654) is made up of nine buildings featuring exhibits on the early Bushman hunter-gatherers, the rise of the Zulu nation and various battles. Two of the buildings were used as dressing rooms during the Battle of Talana. A restored miner's cottage nearby now serves as a restaurant.

Spioenkop

After Isandlwana and Rorke's Drift, Spioenkop is, arguably, the best-known battle in South African history. It took place on 23 and 24 January 1900 after a dismal week for the British, in which attempts to liberate Ladysmith led to their defeats at Magers-fontein, Stormberg and Colenso.

General Redvers Buller, who had positioned himself with 24 000 men and 58 guns on Mount Alice near Spioenkop, managed to cross the Thukela, taking the Boers by surprise, but was again driven back. In a last attempt to win the advantage, he set his sights on capturing Spioenkop, which overlooked the Fairview Road that led to Ladysmith.

The Boer force of 100 men, who had been assigned to protect the summit, fled at the British approach. However, the British made the mistake of digging their trenches at the centre of the summit, which allowed the Boers to climb the hill and counter-attack. Meanwhile, the Boer commander Louis Botha had heard of the British attack and positioned his own men on three surrounding koppies, from where they opened fire on the British position. Both the Boers and the British suffered heavy casualties in the fierce struggle on Spioenkop, and as many as 189 British soldiers were taken prisoner. The Boers reoccupied the summit at dawn the next day.

Today, mass graves stretch from one side of

Mahatma Gandhi, Winston Churchill and Louis Botha, who went on to become prime minister of the Union of South Africa, were all present at the Battle of Spioenkop.

O'Neil's Cottage and Hilldrop House

After the Battle of Majuba, peace negotiations were initiated by Sir Evelyn Wood at O'Neil's Cottage at the foot of Majuba mountain, some 35 kilometres from Newcastle. The house was built by a Catholic, which explains the white cross on the front gable, and was bought by Eugene O'Neil's brother, who later transferred it to him. Some of the wounded from Majuba were cared for in this house. Three men died there and were buried in the nearby orchard.

An armistice was signed at the cottage on 23 March 1881, allowing the Zuid-Afrikaansche Republiek (South African Republic) to retain its independence under the suzerainty of the British. After the truce was signed, the document in respect of retrocession of land to the Boers was signed at Hilldrop House, home of the writer, Sir Rider Haggard.

Hilldrop House is a good example of British rural settlers' use of indigenous yellowwood. Haggard and Arthur Cochran bought the farm on which the house stands in 1879. Cochran farmed there while Haggard returned to Britain to marry. He returned with his wife late in 1880 and, despite the unrest and presence of troops, took up residence at Hilldrop House and remained in the house throughout the hostilities of 1881, farming cattle and ostriches, selling hay and hiring out oxen and wagons to the government. Haggard also built a kiln and established a steam mill. When he let the house to the Royal Commission to discuss the terms of retrocession with the Boer delegation, he retained only one room for the use of his wife. In July of that year, Haggard and Cochran returned to Britain and the house was sold.

Rider Haggard did not write any of his novels while living at Hilldrop House, but his novel *Jess* is based on his experiences while living there, and features ostrich farming and flooded rivers. The farm in the novel, Mooifontein, is easily recognisable, as is Lion Kloof, the hill behind the house.

Spioenkop to the other, marking the position of the British trenches. Three men who would play an important role in world affairs were present on the battlefield that day. They were Louis Botha, the first prime minister of the Union of South Africa; Winston Churchill, who was there as a war correspondent; and Mahatma Gandhi, who was present as a stretcher-bearer.

Visit the battlefields

Six self-drive routes take you to the most important battlefields of northern and central KwaZulu-Natal. Remembrance Route follows the Anglo-Zulu War of 1879, while Rifleman's Road takes you past the key landmarks of the first Anglo-Boer War. For more information contact Tourism Natal (031 366 7500) or Battlefields Route Information (036 352 6253).

The forts

All over KwaZulu-Natal forts were established by the British during this period of conflict with Boer and Zulu. Some have vanished forever. The remains of others are a vivid reminder of the past.

Twin forts: Pearson and Tenedos

Fort Pearson and Fort Tenedos were built across from each other on either side of the mouth of the Thukela in 1878 and 1879, respectively. Nearby the forts, on the northern bank of the Thukela, is Ndonakusuka, where Zulu warriors under Mpande attacked and decimated a force of settlers from Port Natal and several thousand black levies in April 1838. The force had been raised to assist the beleaguered Voortrekker laagers, then under systematic attack by the Zulu. In 1856, Ndonakusuka was also the scene of a great battle between Prince Cetshwayo and his brother, Mbuyazi, the bloodiest battle ever fought on South African soil.

Fort Pearson is named after Colonel Charles Pearson, who led the invasion into Zululand in 1879. It is also the site of the Ultimatum Tree where Cetshwayo was issued the ultimatum intended to spark war. Today, little remains of Fort Pearson apart from the outer trenches.

An earth-walled structure, Fort Tenedos, was named after a British warship that was extensively used throughout the Anglo-Zulu War and served as a garrison and supply base while anchored off the Thukela. The site of the fort is best viewed from Fort Pearson.

kwaMondi/Fort Eshowe

kwaMondi Mission Station in Eshowe was founded in 1869 by Bishop Schreuder of the Norwegian Mission Society. It was commandeered by Colonel Charles Pearson on 23 January 1879, during the Anglo-Zulu War. He renamed the mission Fort Eshowe and used it as a supply depot and hospital. When he heard about the defeat at Isandlwana, Pearson decided to withdraw from Fort Eshowe. Before he could make his move, however, the fort was surrounded and besieged for ten weeks. When the fort was eventually evacuated in April 1879, the Zulu burnt it to the ground. In 1884, it was rebuilt and renamed Fort Curtis.

Fort Durnford

Fort Durnford was built in 1847 on a flat-topped hill near Estcourt that offers a good view of the area, including two drift crossings on the Bushman's River. It was established by a detachment of the 45th Regiment from Fort Napier to protect the Voortrekkers from Bushmen rustlers. The fairly rough original structure was replaced in 1875, in the wake of the Langalibalele rebellion, by a double-storey building of white sandstone.

Fort Durnford is named after Lieutenant Colonel Anthony William Durnford, the officer sent in pursuit of Chief Langalibalele after the amaHlubi defied a British order to register their guns. The building was protected by a stone wall with a two-metre-deep moat around it. Claims that the fort was linked to the Bushman's River by two escape tunnels are unsubstantiated. Although never put to the test, Fort Durnford was thought to be virtually impregnable.

Fort Durnford, which has served not only as a fort but as a girl's reform school and accommodation for teachers, is now a museum.

Fort Nongqai was a base for the Zululand Native Police, who distinguished themselves in the South African War (1899–1902) before their disbandment two years after the end of the war.

Visit Fort Durnford

Until 1927, Fort Durnford was used to house the Bantu Girls' Reform School, which was eventually moved to Estcourt. In 1960, it was used as accommodation for teachers attached to the local government school. These days the fort is a museum, the main exhibit featuring the fort itself and its fascinating defence mechanisms. There is also a reconstructed Amangwane Zulu kraal on the grounds. The museum is open Monday to Sunday from 09h00 to noon and from 13h00 to 16h00.

Nongqai Fort

The Zululand Native Police force was formed in 1883 as a bodyguard to protect the Resident Commissioner of Zululand, Sir Melmoth Osborne. The force was led by Colonel Mansel, who had served with the Natal Mounted Police, and it recruited its members from among the black population. Its members were generally known as the Nongqai (thought to be a Zulu rendition of 'non-white') and operated from Fort Nongqai.

Fort Nongqai was established on the boundary of Eshowe in 1883 in a location that commanded a view in all directions. Two drifters claiming to be tradesmen were initially commissioned to build the fort, but they were sent packing when it became obvious that they were not what they claimed to be. The walls they built were pulled down and work on the building was begun from scratch. The fort, when it was finally built, was three storeys high, roughly L-shaped, with three turrets, of two storeys each, at the corners. Each turret has six square metres of parapet roof, cement stairs and loopholes for defence.

The Nongqai served with distinction, not least in the South African War (1899–1902), before the unit was disbanded without warning in 1904. When they were recalled in 1906, at the time of the Bhambatha uprising, 120 former members responded. The unit was disbanded again afterwards.

Until recently, the magazine of the South African Police was named *Nongqai* in honour of the unit. The fort was used by the Provincial Roads Department before it was turned into a museum.

Towns and surrounds

Of the towns in this part of KwaZulu-Natal, Ladysmith, Greytown and Newcastle contain some notable sites in KwaZulu-Natal's history and heritage.

Ladysmith

On 2 November 1899, not long after the Battle of Elandslaagte, the Boer forces under the leadership of General Piet Joubert besieged Ladysmith. The town, which is named after the wife of the former governor of the Cape Colony, Sir Harry Smith, is known mainly for the siege and the battles that were fought in the surrounding hills. Ladysmith is notable also for its association with Mahatma Gandhi. With the Indian ambulance corps he had organised, Gandhi contributed towards the relief of Ladysmith, himself serving

The Siege Museum commemorates the most notable event in Ladysmith's history, the Siege of Ladysmith.

as a stretcher-bearer with Buller's relief column. There is a memorial to Gandhi in the Vishnu Bhagwan temple in Forbes Street.

Established in 1847, Ladysmith was the largest town in the Klip River district and an important stopover for transport wagons on the route between Natal and the Transvaal. During the 118-day-long siege, the stone town hall sustained considerable damage. It has since been restored to the original vision created by architects Walker and Singleton in 1893. Its imposing symmetrical façade and portico are supported by four columns in the Italian Renaissance style. A clock tower rises above the roof with an Eastern-inspired cupola that is typical of late-Victorian public buildings.

Inhabitants of the town sheltered from Boer artillery fire under the banks of the Klip River and, later, in a neutral area downstream which became known as Intombi camp. In a lighter moment on Christmas Day, the Boers fired a shell containing a Christmas pudding into the town. The siege ended on 28 February 1900 when a relief column under General Buller finally managed to fight its way through the Boer lines and into the town.

Visit the Siege Museum

Located next to the Town Hall, the building housing the Siege Museum (036 637 2231) was erected in 1884. It was used as a rations post for civilians. The museum houses a three-dimensional model depicting Ladysmith at the time of the siege. It displays relics from the time of the siege, including documents, uniforms and firearms.

Greytown

Founded on 31 December 1853, Greytown would have been named Pretorius after the Voortrekker leader Andries Pretorius who had borne arms against the British, had the name not been overruled by the colonial authorities.

Pastor Louis Harms established the Hermannsburg Lutheran Church at Greytown in September 1854. The church is closely associated with the German settlers in Natal. When it became too small for the congregation, a German settler

The Indian presence at Ladysmith
Ladysmith contains several Hindu and Muslim places of worship.

Hindu Thirukootam and Shri Ganaser Temple
In the early 1880s, a small Hindu temple constructed of wood and iron in Ladysmith's old railway barracks was used for daily worship and observances of important pujas (ceremonial offerings). In 1915, the mother of V S Pillay, a prominent member of the community, donated a piece of land for the establishment of a new temple and hall. In 1916, Alaga Pillay, a famous master builder, who had been brought in from India to build the Vishnu Temple in Durban, was commissioned to build Ladysmith's Hindu Thirukootam and Shri Ganaser Temple.

The buildings are a fine example of the integration of colonial verandah-style buildings with traditional Indian temple form. Pillay's chosen dome form and sculpture remained unchanged, however, never venturing beyond the naive quality of the lotus dome, which he used in the Umgeni Temple, built in Durban.

Improvements to the temple were made over the years. Although a Tamil school was already in existence in 1910, the new temple hall became the venue for classes in 1916. The temple is still used for daily services and Hindu festivals. The area, however, has become a busy business district and a new temple is planned.

The Sufi mosque
Hazrath Soofi Saheb, a prominent South African Muslim cleric, founded 12 mosques while he lived in the country, one of them being the beautiful Sufi mosque on the bank of the Klip River in Ladysmith (below). The mosque was built sometime between 1895 and 1910, but was expanded in the mid-1960s. Much of the original building still exists, although incorporated into the newer structure.

Jamaloodeen, the mosque's master builder, learnt his trade from his father and grandfather and is said to have designed the building in his head, sketching plans for the day's work onto a smoothed area of sand each morning. No other plans for the building exist. Its architectural style integrates traditional Muslim design with building material and structural systems typical of the 1960s. The ornamental plasterwork is of particularly good craftsmanship and of unusually high quality. Much of the additional ornamentation is of prefabricated asbestos cement, and the verandahs and balconies are lined with typical 1960s honeycomb brickwork.

from East London built a larger church with the help of the colonists who had arrived with the missionaries. The church took two years to build and was finally completed in 1870. The yellow-wood timber used in its construction was cut from the Matimolo forests, about 20 kilometres from the church. German, Boer, English and Zulus alike attended the opening service. Two years later, after days of soaking rain, the foundations of the tall tower collapsed. A new steeple was erected, which was smaller than the original. During the Anglo-Zulu War in 1879, the windows of the church were barricaded and it was used as a fortress and place of safety. Greytown never came under attack by the Zulu. Nevertheless, the sick and the ill were carried into the church at night whenever the situation became tense.

On the southern edge of Greytown, on a little farm called Honeyfontein, is a cairn marking the birthplace of Louis Botha, a soldier who was the first prime minister of the Union of South Africa. Botha enjoyed a long career as a politician and worked tirelessly to reconcile the opposing Boer and British groups. He died of a heart attack shortly after returning from the Versailles Peace Conference in 1919.

Bhambatha Rock

This monument was erected in memory of Chief Bhambatha kaJangeni uMancinza Zondi, who led a protest in 1906 against a tax levied on the black peasantry by Natal's colonial authorities. It is located next to the very rock where Bhambatha ambushed members of the Natal Mounted Police who were escorting civilians to safety in Greytown on 4 April 1906. The rock lies 23 kilometres

from Greytown on the road to Keate's Drift. Alongside is a memorial to the four policemen that were killed in the ambush.

Although the poll tax issued in 1905 applied to adults of all races, it hit the impoverished black communities the hardest. Most tribal chiefs refused to collect the tax, saying either that their people did not have the money or that they needed more time. In response, the government sent 170 members of the Natal Mounted Police to Mpanza to arrest Chief Bhambatha of the amaZondi whom they believed to be leading the resistance. Bhambatha fled to King Dinuzulu's kraal at uSuthu. When he returned, he found that the British authorities had deposed him and installed his uncle as chief. Bhambatha quickly regained power and this time round he did organise a resistance force.

Bhambatha and his men were trapped and killed by colonial forces in the Mome Gorge. This engagement virtually ended the rebellion, which had led to the death of approximately 3 500 people. The Bhambatha uprising is considered a forerunner of the freedom struggle in South Africa.

Newcastle

Newcastle was the fourth town to be established in Natal. It was founded in 1864 and was named after the Duke of Newcastle. The town played a strategic role in both phases of the Anglo-Boer War and is home to the Old Armoury as well as one of the country's 12 Carnegie Libraries, which were funded by the American billionaire philanthropist, Andrew Carnegie. The site chosen for the Carnegie Library was once an old jail, as

Maria Ratschitz Mission

Slightly south of Karel Landman's house, on the edge of the Biggarsberg, is the Maria Ratschitz Mission. Established in 1889 by two Trappist monks, it is currently owned by the Catholic Church.

Once a vibrant centre, the mission fell into disrepair when the community it served began to be affected by apartheid laws. Having barely survived the repercussions of the 1913 Land Act, the mission struggled on until the 1960s and early 1970s, when hundreds of people were forcibly removed from the area. By 1975, without a viable community to serve, there was no longer a resident priest and the mission buildings began to fall into disrepair.

In the wake of political change in the early 1990s, the mission was redeveloped and began to play a role in the lives of the growing numbers of people who returned to the area. The magnificent cathedral has been restored to its former glory; its spire stands tall in the rolling hills and the bells again ring out across the farmlands.

Groutville: Luthuli's town

The grave of Chief John Albert Mvumbi Luthuli, leading political figure and Nobel Peace Prizewinner, is found in Groutville, just south of Stanger/KwaDukuza.

Born in Rhodesia in 1898, Luthuli was the son of a missionary. When his father died in 1904, he went to stay with his family in Groutville, where he learnt Zulu traditions in the house of his uncle, Martin Luthuli, chief of the abaSematholweni and a founder of the African National Congress (ANC). He was educated at Adams Mission south of Durban. He later lectured at the mission under the activist Z K Matthews until 1935, when his uncle died and he was elected chief. He then returned to Groutville, where he became prominent in the Congregational Church and chair of the Natal Missions Board. He was also a successful farmer, chairing the Zulu Cane Growers' Association.

Luthuli first ventured into politics when he joined the short-lived Native Representative Council. In 1943, he joined the ANC, partially out of frustration at the land acts that had been passed. By 1945, he was on the Natal executive of the ANC. In 1951, he replaced W G Champion as the party leader in the province, coordinating the Defiance Campaign in Natal. In 1952, he became president of the ANC, a post he held until his death.

During his time in office, Albert Luthuli was instrumental in placing the ANC on a more militant footing. Luthuli was a reluctant convert to violence, which he saw as the unavoidable consequence of apartheid, favouring instead sanctions as the next line of protest.

Although the government restricted his movements to Groutville during the last years of his life, Luthuli nonetheless managed to lead the Kliptown Congress of People in the drafting of the Freedom Charter in 1955. From Groutville, he coordinated the increasing number of ANC-sponsored boycotts, strikes and Pass Book protests. He was detained from 1956–57 and was imprisoned when the ANC was banned in 1960. In 1961, he was awarded the Nobel Peace Prize.

Luthuli remained a mentor of the ANC's underground movement until his death in mysterious circumstances on 21 July 1967. His grave, located at his family home in Groutville, has been declared a national monument. A large black granite slab with a simple cross and a short inscription marks the grave. At the foot are two vases inscribed with the names of his two daughters, who, in exile at the time of his death, were unable to attend his funeral.

Luthuli's family home was originally built of mud in 1927, but over the years parts have been renovated and upgraded. It is now a colonial/Union-vernacular home of plastered brick with a corrugated-iron roof and a verandah supported by plastered brick piers. Some of the interior walls are wattle and daub. There are plans to open sections of the house to the public in order to display memorabilia relating to Albert Luthuli's life.

evidenced by the cells found there. The finished library, a typically Edwardian-style building, was officially opened in 1915.

It is thought that the Old Armoury was built by the Newcastle Mounted Rifles, a volunteer mounted corps that came into being after 1854 and was established in response to growing fear of Zulu attack. Settlers as far north as Barberton and Wakkerstroom feared that Cetshwayo would try to reclaim Zulu territory. The armoury is like a small fort fitted with a firing platform and rifle turrets to protect the troops manning it. Weapons were stored behind exceptionally strong security doors imported from Britain.

Troops at the armoury were placed on alert during the Anglo-Boer Wars and in the 1906 Bhambatha uprising. During World War I, Newcastle's armoury was an important mobilisation centre for troops that served in South-West Africa, now Namibia. In 1939, the armoury was again called into service as a post for soldiers signing up for World War II. It is a monument of sorts to the volunteer regiments of South Africa.

KZN South

Although there is evidence to suggest that Phoenician navigators put in at present-day Durban for fresh supplies as long ago as 700 BC, the first reliable written record of Durban dates back to 1497, when Portuguese explorer Vasco da Gama sighted land on Christmas Day and named it Terra de Natalia. In the 400 years that followed, the tidal lagoon was variously called eThekwini, Ponta de Pescario, Rio de Natal and Port Natal, before it became known as Durban Bay. Durban is one of the few natural ports along South Africa's eastern coastline.

Merchants and sailors used the beautiful lagoon as a stopover for supplies for nearly 350 years before the first European settlers began to arrive in the 1820s. The area was thick with water birds, and elephants would lumber down through the trees to the wetlands around the bay. The lagoon provided humans with a relatively safe haven, fresh water and food. It teemed with fish and – almost unbelievably, now that it is the site of one of Africa's largest and busiest ports – was home to flamingos, fish eagles, coastal elephants, hippopotami, buffaloes and a host of other wild animals.

South of Durban, the strip of coast towards Port Edward on the Eastern Cape border, has become synonymous with holidays filled with sun and the warm surf typical of South Africa's eastern shores. One has only to scratch the surface, however, to find evidence of the area's rich history. Stately old homes and the wrecks of Portuguese galleons whisper of bygone eras in which trade was a tool of colonisation, survival depended on agricultural success and religion held communities together – and set them apart – as the frontiers of colonial Natal gradually moved south.

The beautiful lagoon sighted by Vasco da Gama on Christmas Day in 1497 is now a bustling harbour.

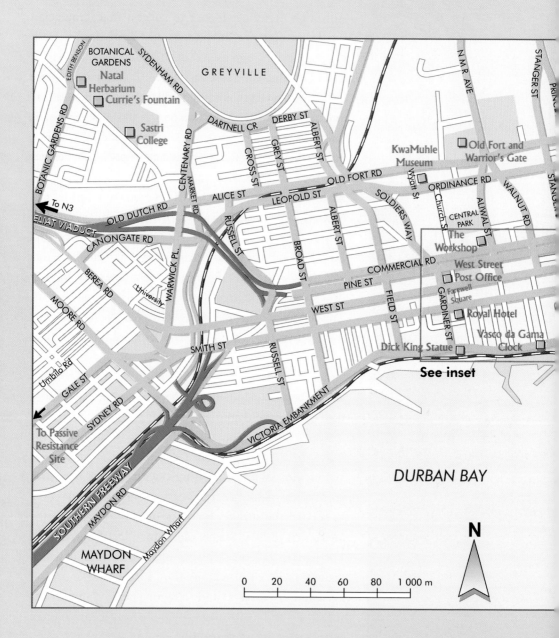

BOTANICAL
GARDENS
EDITH BENSON
Natal
Herbarium
Currie's Fountain
SYDENHAM RD

GREYVILLE

Sastri
College

BOTANIC GARDENS RD

CENTENARY RD

DARTNELL CR

DERBY ST

ALBERT ST

CROSS ST

GREY ST

MARKET RD

ALICE ST

LEOPOLD ST

OLD FORT RD

KwaMuhle
Museum

Wyatt St

Old Fort and
Warrior's Gate

ORDINANCE RD

N M R AVE

STANGER ST

PRINCE

STANGER

WALNUT RD

To N3

ELIAT VIADUCT

OLD DUTCH RD

CANONGATE RD

WARWICK PL

RUSSELL ST

BROAD ST

ALBERT ST

SOLDIERS WAY

Church St

CENTRAL
PARK

ALWAL ST

The
Workshop

BEREA RD

University

MOORE RD

COMMERCIAL RD

PINE ST

WEST ST

FIELD ST

West Street
Post Office
Farewell
Square

GARDINER ST

Royal Hotel

Vasco da Gama
Clock

Umbilo Rd

GALE ST

SYDNEY RD

SMITH ST

RUSSELL ST

Dick King Statue

See inset

To Passive
Resistance
Site

VICTORIA EMBANKMENT

DURBAN BAY

SOUTHERN FREEWAY

MAYDON RD

Maydon Wharf

MAYDON
WHARF

0   20   40   60   80   1 000 m

N

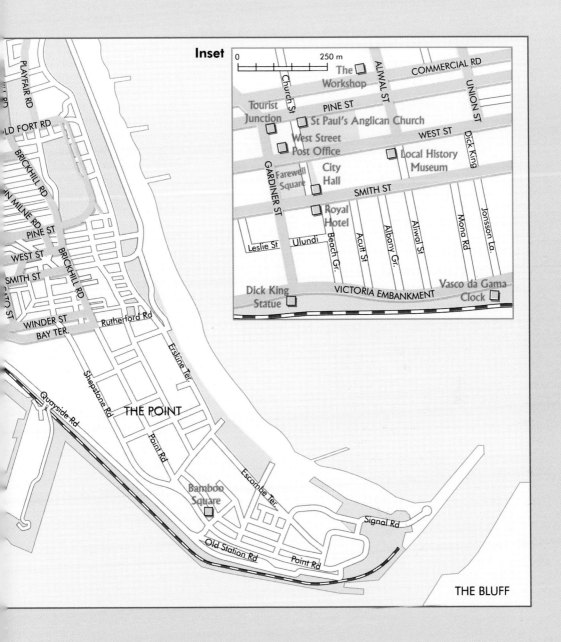

Inset

0   250 m

THE WORKSHOP

COMMERCIAL RD

ALIWAL ST

UNION ST

Church St

PINE ST

Tourist
Junction

St Paul's Anglican Church

West Street
Post Office

WEST ST

Dick King

Local History
Museum

GARDINER ST

Farewell
Square

City
Hall

SMITH ST

Royal
Hotel

Leslie St   Ulundi

Beach Gr.

Acuff St

Albany Gr.

Aliwal St

Mona Rd

Jonsson La.

Dick King
Statue

VICTORIA EMBANKMENT

Vasco da Gama
Clock

PLAYFAIR RD

LD FORT RD

BRICKHILL RD

N MILNE RD

PINE ST

WEST ST

SMITH ST

BRICKHILL RD

WINDER ST

BAY TER.

Rutherford Rd

Quayside Rd

Shepstone Rd

THE POINT

Erskine Ter.

Point Rd

Escombe Ter.

Bamboo
Square

Signal Rd

Old Station Rd

Point Rd

THE BLUFF

Durban: port of many nations

Since the 1820s, when the likes of Francis George Farewell, Henry Francis Fynn and James King sought to open trade in ivory with the Zulu, traders, missionaries, wars, settlers and harbour engineers have all played a significant role in altering the landscape around Durban Bay. In those early years there existed a fairly amicable trading relationship, which changed after King Dingane's attacks on the Voortrekkers who were looking to settle in the Natal highlands. Although Dingane viewed the area of Durban as Zulu territory, he mostly refrained from attacking the port because his attention was focused on the greater threat posed by the Voortrekkers.

While war between Zulu, Boer and British continued inland in the course of the 19th century, Durban grew apace. It was annexed by the British authorities in the Cape in 1843. Fifty years later, it had taken shape as a major trade centre, with the introduction of the first electric trams and

ongoing development of the harbour. Today, Durban is one of Africa's largest and busiest ports. This cultural melting pot is also home to the largest population of Indians outside of India.

City and suburbs

In 1824, Francis Farewell and Henry Fynn set up a trading camp on what became Market Square, part of which is now known as Farewell Square in the hub of the city. Fynn and Farewell traded ivory and other items with the Zulu under the rule of Shaka. Soon their little trading post grew into a settlement of wattle-and-daub houses made with mangrove poles harvested from the edge of the bay as their salt content made them resistant to termites. Difficult as it is for us to imagine today, their camp lay in a great coastal forest of milkwood, mahogany, umdoni and enormous wild fig trees.

Farewell Square

As one would expect, many of the most prominent of Durban's commercial and religious institutions grew up around Market (now Farewell) Square. The first courthouse (now the Local History Museum), the well-known Royal Hotel, City Hall and West Street Post Office were all built on or around Market Square. Many still serve their original purpose.

Farewell Square is one of the few open spaces in the centre of Durban and the only open area that remains of the original square. It is planted with large indigenous trees, making it a favourite spot for office workers to enjoy lunch.

Commemorations

From the front steps on the City Hall, across the pedestrian promenade formerly known as Church Street (because of the location of St Paul's Church in the street), two plaques can be seen on the wall surrounding Farewell Square. They commemorate Durban's first centenary and were unveiled in 1924 by Princess Alice, Countess of Athlone, who was the wife of the Governor-General. Two smaller plaques were erected in 1974 to mark the province's 150th anniversary.

A statue of Queen Victoria was erected in the square in 1887 to commemorate the queen's golden jubilee. In 1909, a cast-iron fountain that stood in the square near Queen Victoria's statue was moved to the beachfront – where it promptly rusted away. All that remains are the plaques that were relocated to the base of the statue.

Not far off stands a monument to the men from the city who died during the South African War of 1899–1902. Facing the City Hall are the statues of Harry Escombe (attorney and second prime minister of Natal) and Sir John Robinson (newspaperman, politician and first prime minister of Natal). There is also a cenotaph and a wall of remembrance in honour of the men of Durban who fell in the two World Wars.

City Hall

Durban's City Hall, completed in 1910, lies on the eastern side of Farewell Square. Although this is not obvious from the outside, the City Hall is actually four separate buildings with three main entrances, one of which leads to a massive public hall with an enormous organ, wooden floors and elaborate roof carvings.

The building's Edwardian, neo-baroque façade is complemented by allegorical sculptures depicting the arts, music, literature, commerce and industry. Stories about these sculptures abound. According to one, they are the city's earliest public depictions of nudity – hardly scandalous since the modesty of most of the figures is protected by strategically placed clothing or leaves. Legend has it that one of the building contractors, Jack Hollis, used his small sons as models for the cherubs. One of the sons, George Hollis, became Durban's mayor in 1976, no doubt the only mayor in history with nude sculptures of himself adorning his premises.

Interestingly, the City Hall is the first public building in South Africa to depict a black man; he can be seen crouching, shield in hand, in the right-hand corner of the frieze over the Church Street entrance. There is also, supposedly, an Indian woman in the same frieze. If so, she is well hidden. At the time of construction of the building, there was much debate in government as to whether Indians who had entered the Colony as indentured labourers should be allowed to remain in the country or be shipped back to India.

Visit City Hall

Durban's City Hall houses the Council Chambers and Town Clerk's offices, as well as the Durban Art Gallery, Natural History Museum and General Lending Library. All are well worth a visit and tours can be arranged through Durban Africa at Tourist Junction, or through staff at the Cultural History Museum, who can also take you on a fascinating city-centre walkabout.

Allegorical sculptures adorn Durban's City Hall.

St Paul's Anglican Church and the Vicarage

On the corner of Church Square, between the Post Office and the old public baths (now, sadly, closed and facing an insecure future) you will find a number of enormous, gnarled wild fig trees that would surely have some amazing tales to tell if they could talk. It is a credit to city managers that they have managed to maintain and protect these living relics against all odds. Perhaps these wild figs lasted as long as they have because they are situated next to the original location of St Paul's Anglican Church.

Unlike most of Durban's Catholic churches and missions, which are located away from the city centre – possibly as a result of underlying prejudice against Catholics by the city's predominantly Protestant forefathers – St Paul's Anglican Church was built right on the square. In 1906 the church burned down and the vicarage was erected in its stead. For a while, the vicarage was used as Durban's tourism office.

St Paul's is probably the most historic church in the city centre and features lovely old stained-glass windows and a large nave terminating in a well-appointed sanctuary. It contains memorial tablets that record much of Durban's history.

The wild fig trees in the city centre are protected as national monuments.

Royal Hotel

The Royal Hotel was built of wattle and daub in 1847. Then called the Commercial Hotel, its name was changed to the Masonic Hotel in 1848, when it became a meeting place for Freemasons. It was only in 1860, after a visit by Prince Alfred, son of Queen Victoria, that it was renamed the Royal Hotel. It has been rebuilt three times and has hosted such illustrious guests as Rudyard Kipling, Mark Twain, Rider Haggard, H G Wells and Cecil John Rhodes.

West Street Post Office

The beautiful West Street Post Office on the edge of Farewell Square was completed in 1885 in accordance with the winning designs of architect Philip Dudgeon. The building initially doubled as Durban's (first) city hall, postal agency and museum. The building soon became too small to serve all these functions for the burgeoning port city and construction of the present city hall began in 1905. The first session of the National Convention, which formulated the Union of South Africa, met in the West Street Post Office in 1908. Even though extensively changed at the rear, the building remains one of South Africa's finest classical structures.

Although dwarfed by Durban's modern architecture, West Street Post Office retains its dignity.

Local History Museum

As the town grew, buildings were put up around Market Square, of which the oldest surviving structure is the courthouse on Aliwal Street. It was opened in 1863, and now serves as the Local History Museum.

During the boom years of the 1880s, a second storey and small turret were added, making the building one of the tallest in the southern hemisphere until it was surpassed by the West Street Post Office in 1885. The building was taken over by the Durban Corporation in 1910, and has housed the museum since 1965.

These days, the ground floor of the museum hosts a changing display of Durban's early fashions. To the right are a little museum shop and an interesting exhibition of the history of soccer in South Africa and Durban – not quite a dusty old colonial exhibition! At the top of a wide wooden staircase is an audio-visual display of statuettes of movers and shakers in Durban's history. Here Gandhi stands alongside the Shembes – leaders of the Shembe Church – and Albert Luthuli. At the touch of a button, you can learn about the role they and other personalities played in Durban's development.

The museum contains a beautifully reconstructed Victorian haberdashery, as well as an excellent depiction of Henry Fynn's settler shack on The Bluff. A model of Fynn sits outside a dimly-lit wattle-and-daub hut in much the same way Fynn may himself have done back in 1824 when he set up a thriving trade in ivory, hippopotamus tusks and buffalo hides with the Zulu. The model conveys a sense of the living conditions of Durban's early settlers.

Visit the Local History Museum

The Local History Museum (031 311 2223) is a great place to while away a windy or wet afternoon while learning about early Durban and the characters who shaped this vibrant African city. It is open Monday to Saturday from 08h30 to 16h00 and Sundays and public holidays from 11h00 to 16h00.

The Local History Museum is housed in the oldest surviving building in Durban's city centre.

The Old Railway Buildings:
Tourist Junction and The Workshop

Durban's Tourist Junction is housed in what was once the administration block of the Central Railway Station. The building still bears the letters 'N G R' (Natal Government Railways). Part of the rear of the old railway station and the link to the main platform shed were demolished when Commercial Road was extended.

The Old Railway Buildings have been converted into a tourist information centre with a coffee shop and an art gallery.

Constructed in 1894 by designer William Street Wilson, the railway buildings acquired two more storeys in 1904. From the dolphin motif in the carved stone balustrade to the first-floor verandah, it would appear that, even in the early part of the previous century, Durbanites were conscious of their association with the sea and marine life.

In 1986, the locomotive shed across the road from the old railway station was remodelled into a shopping complex, retaining much of the building's wonderful architecture. Five massive doors on the south façade that once gave locomotives access to the cavernous interior now lead to a variety of shops. The interior still has an industrial feel, with many of the metal spans left exposed.

Outside are sprawling lawns and trees and a small amphitheatre with a mosaic fountain designed by Andrew Verster, a resident of Durban and one of South Africa's leading artists.

Tourist Junction is centrally situated and is a good starting point for walking tours of the city's Indian district on the Oriental Walkabout or for the Historical Walkabout. It houses the offices of Durban Africa, Durban's tourism marketing division; KwaZulu-Natal Tourism; the booking and information office of Ezemvelo KZN Wildlife; and the African Art Centre.

KwaMuhle Museum

The building that now houses the KwaMuhle Museum plays a fundamental, if ignominious, role in South Africa's history. Once the notorious Department of Native Affairs, Durban's colonial authorities refined the principles and structures of urban racial segregation – the blueprint of South Africa's abhorrent apartheid policy – within these walls.

Ironically, *kwaMuhle* means 'Place of the Good One'. In this case, the 'Good One' was John S Marwick, who earned his Zulu praise name when he marched 7 000 Zulu labourers from the Transvaal goldfields home to safety at the out-break of the South African War in 1899. Marwick went on to manage the first Native Administration Department, and the name *kwaMuhle* stuck to the premises.

Today, the displays in the KwaMuhle Museum provide a fascinating and sometimes heartbreaking glimpse of the city's apartheid past and the misery and indignities caused by laws that rendered the

The offices of the notorius Department of Native Affairs were housed in what is now the KwaMuhle Museum.

majority of the population second-class citizens in the country of their birth. The exhibits also offer background to the plans that were outlined within the building, such as the imposition of segregation, the creation of townships and single-sex worker compounds, and the issuing of orders to 'sheep-dip' all Africans entering the town for fear of disease. A particularly interesting permanent exhibit depicts the history of Cato Manor, an area that once experienced traumatic forced removals and is now a sprawling informal settlement behind the Berea.

Ironically, because all Africans seeking work in Durban first had to pass through the corridors of the Department of Native Affairs, KwaMuhle became something of a social hub in the city.

Old Fort at Warrior's Gate

The Old Fort marks the site of the British camp besieged by the Boers in 1842. A 237-man British force under Captain Thomas Charlton Smith held out in the camp for 34 days against the Boers, under Commandant-General Andries Pretorius. In the mean time, Dick King rode to Grahamstown for reinforcements. Their arrival led to the lifting of the siege and the annexation of Natal by Britain.

Originally known as Fort Itafa Amalinde, the fort was used as the headquarters of various British regiments until 1897. Its barracks and a guardroom date back to 1858, and a magazine that was part of the original structure is now used as a chapel. The well that supplied the garrison, the original farrier's workshop and the bell tower, from which hangs the bell of HMS *Durban*, are still to be seen. There is also a Garden of Remembrance with a World War I field gun.

Visit the Old Fort

A museum containing battlefield relics, medals, badges and other militaria is housed near the Old Fort at Warrior's Gate (031 307 3337), headquarters of the MOTHS (Memorable Order of the Tin Hats), an association of old servicemen. The Gate was built in 1937 in remembrance of all who have fallen in the service of their country. The museum is open Tuesday to Sunday from 11h00 to 15h00 and Saturday from 10h00 to 12h00.

A model of the original fort as well as other military memorabilia can be seen at the Old Fort.

The Vasco da Gama Clock, a beautifully elaborate wrought-iron structure on the Victoria Embankment, was donated to the city by Durban's Portuguese community.

Vasco da Gama Clock

An ornate clock located on the Victoria Embankment, close to the harbour, commemorates the Portuguese explorer, Vasco da Gama, who first sighted Durban Bay in 1497. Durban's Portuguese community donated the clock to the city on the 400th anniversary of Da Gama's arrival. It was originally installed in Point Road in 1897, but later moved to its present – and perhaps more appropriate – location on the leafy sidewalk on Victoria Embankment. A small stone plaque next to the clock marking the 500th anniversary of Da Gama's birth was unveiled in 1969 by the Portuguese ambassador.

Dick King Statue

Much has been written and a movie made about the romantic figure of Dick King, a 17-year-old boy who rode the gruelling 970 kilometres from Port Natal to Grahamstown in 1842 in just ten days. Dick King and his servant, Ndongeni, set out for Grahamstown to obtain assistance for the British troops besieged by the Boers in Durban's Old Fort. A large statue of Dick King stands at the corner of Gardiner Street and Victoria Embankment, atop a plinth with two bronze plaques commemorating the ride.

King continued to live in Durban as a hunter, trader and butcher. A plaque marks the location of his shop at the corner of Smith and Dick King Streets, east of the main thoroughfare, Aliwal Street, at a short distance from what was then Market Square.

The Dick King statue commemorates one of the many fascinating characters in Durban's history.

Preserving our natural heritage

The Natal Agricultural and Horticultural Society was founded in 1848 for experimentation purposes. In 1851, the Society laid out the Durban Botanical Gardens. When John Medley Wood was appointed curator in 1882, he took the position on condition that he be allowed to develop a Herbarium. The Herbarium ceased to be part of the Botanical Gardens in 1913, when it was given to the Durban Corporation. Medley Wood died in 1915, having made a significant contribution to botanical knowledge in South Africa. Medwood Gardens, in the city centre, are named for him. Today, the Natal Herbarium houses a valuable collection of more than 75 000 plant specimens.

There are two buildings of architectural interest on this site: the Herbarium, which houses the institution's collections, and Medley Wood House, which was the curator's residence and is now used for office accommodation.

Natal Herbarium

The present Herbarium replaced an earlier wood-and-iron structure and was completed in 1902. It consists of a large specimen storage area flanked by two gable-ended wings. Between the wings, on both sides of the building, are verandahs. A notable feature is the double staircase leading up to the front verandah. The building is decorated in the classical style, with pediment gable ends and a verandah colonnade.

Medley Wood House

Medley Wood House was built in 1889 at a cost of £940. A significant example of the architecture of its period, it has a complex roofline and a large central bay window around which the verandah projects. The decorative wooden trimmings are unusual in terms of both scale and pattern.

The Herbarium and Medley Wood House are both built in red brick, which is not very common in Durban. The brick used differs noticeably from the better-known Pietermaritzburg and Dundee varieties.

Visit the Natal Herbarium

The Herbarium is adjacent to the Durban Botanical Gardens and is open to visitors by appointment from Mondays to Fridays, 07h45 to 16h30. Call 031 202 4095 to book a time or for more information.

Bamboo Square

Earth works for construction of Durban's new Point Development and uShaka Island Theme Park and Aquarium brought to light the ruins of Bamboo Square, a shantytown that was burned down at the beginning of the last century following an outbreak of bubonic plague. Its inhabitants were forcibly relocated. The plague, which was brought to Durban by a passing ship, resulted in 124 deaths.

The Point Development was halted while the site was excavated. The archaeological find has since been incorporated into the design of the new development and will be open for public viewing.

Sastri College

As a result of an agreement in 1926 between the Government of India and the Union of South Africa, the Indian Enquiry Commission was appointed to investigate the matter of Indian education in Natal. Until then, the Indian community had to rely on its own financial resources to meet the educational needs of Indian children.

Sastri College was built in 1928 on land adjoining Currie's Fountain that was donated by the Durban City Council. When it opened in 1930, it was the first Indian high school in South Africa and, although built primarily to provide secondary education for Indian boys, it soon became a centre for teacher training. In 1936, part-time university classes for 'students of colour' were held by Natal University College at Sastri College.

Sastri College is of architectural as well as historical and cultural significance. The double-storey building is designed in the Berea style of the Union period, with hipped tile roofs, a projecting entrance portico and arcades on two floors on the main-entrance elevation. Over the years, various additions have been made to the rear of the original block.

At one stage, it was decided that Sastri College would be incorporated into the former M L Sultan College, now part of the Durban Institute of Technology. However, Dr A D Lazarus, the school's principal at the time, lobbied furiously to have the college declared a national monument as the most effective way to ensure that it would remain in its original form.

Outlying areas and suburbs
Elephant House

Reputedly the first house built on the Berea, Elephant House dates back to 1849 and is, possibly, the oldest remaining colonial-period house in Durban. It takes its name from the many elephants that used to pass by the old house on their way from Springfield Flats and Sea Cow Lake to the Bayside swamps.

Elephant House is of architectural as well as historic interest. It is a low, rectangular cottage with a typical Natal verandah which retains the original woodwork. It now has windows on the front façade and French doors with narrow glazing. Asbestos sheets have replaced the original corrugated-iron roof.

Sastri College was the first high school for Indian boys in KwaZulu-Natal.

University of Natal: Howard College and Memorial Tower Building

Howard College and the Memorial Tower on the Durban campus of the University of Natal are well-known landmarks, easily seen from the air and recognisable from across the bay. Howard College, completed in 1931, is the oldest building on the campus. Viewed from the east, the building, which consists of a centrally placed rotunda facing elegant columns and a balustrade, is said to resemble Senate House at the University of London.

Planning for the Memorial Tower building, the second-oldest building on campus, began at the end of World War II, some years before Natal University College became a fully-fledged university. Construction was completed between 1947 and 1950. Originally known as the Science and Technology Block, the building's reading-room tower was later crowned with the Light of Remembrance that would be 'visible from far out at sea to serve as a reminder of the Fallen in the two World Wars' and – on a more pragmatic note – would serve as a navigational beacon.

Howard College, one of Durban's most famous landmarks, has been declared a national monument.

DURBAN: OUTLYING AREAS & SUBURBS

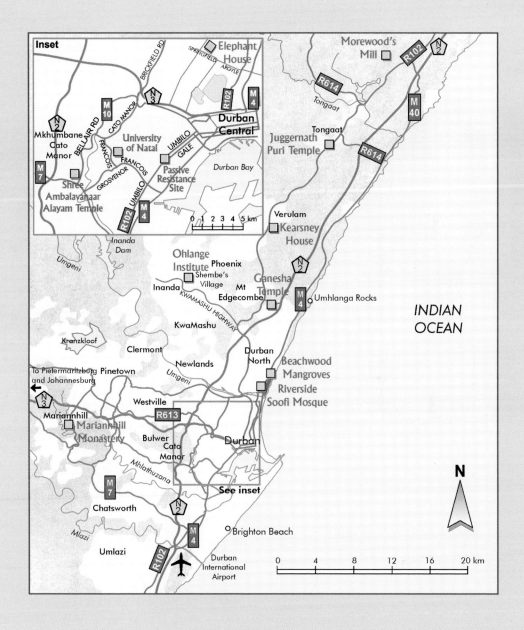

In 1946, 15 000 people marched to where the Passive Resistance Site is now situated, in a campaign of resistance against apartheid.

Passive Resistance Site

This site, in a park at the intersection of Umbilo Road and Gale Street, symbolises the start of the second Passive Resistance Campaign by the Indian community of KwaZulu-Natal, from 1946 to 1948. The campaign, inspired by Mahatma Gandhi's doctrine of passive resistance, was organised in response to the Asiatic Land Tenure and Indian Representation Act. The Act prohibited Indians from buying land and occupying territory except in certain 'exempted areas', and restricted Indian representation in parliament to a communal franchise. On 13 June 1946, the Natal Indian Congress, led by Dr Monty Naiker, with the support of the Transvaal Indian Congress under Dr Yusuf Dadoo, held a mass meeting at Red Square to launch a campaign of passive resistance against the 'Ghetto Act'. After the meeting, a crowd of 15 000 Natal Indian Congress supporters marched to the intersection of Umbilo Road and Gale Street and the first batch of 18 volunteers, led by Dr Naiker and M D Naidoo, courted arrest by pitching five tents on a vacant lot owned by the Durban Municipality. Police were forced to intervene when a gang of white youths attacked the group, cutting ropes, tearing down tents and threatening the passive resisters. By June 1948, when the Natal Indian Congress suspended the campaign, more than 2 200 Indian men and women had been arrested, tried and imprisoned.

Riots at Cato Manor

Cato Manor, also known as Mkhumbane, is well known for the riots of 1949 and 1959–60. In 1960, thousands of Africans demanding the release of detained ANC activists set out from Cato Manor and tried to reach the central jail in the city centre along various routes. When police blocked them, the marchers turned violent and many Indian shops were looted, vandalised or burned. Only about 1 000 demonstrators reached the central jail.

The suburb, about two kilometres east of the city, was once home to a vibrant mix of Indian and African families. However, the residents were moved off the land under the infamous Group Areas Act and resettled, some as far away as KwaMashu, and their homes destroyed. A few colourful Hindu temples and small mosques were all that stood in the overgrown vegetation for many years. People slowly began to settle again on the vacant land, turning Cato Manor into a sprawling informal settlement. It is currently the focus of one of the country's most ambitious urban renewal programmes.

Shree Ambalavanaar Alayam Temple

The Shree Ambalavanaar Alayam Temple in Bellair Road, Cato Manor, was the first Hindu temple to be built in Africa. Erected in 1875 on the banks of the Umbilo River, it was damaged beyond repair during floods in 1905. The present structure was built in Bellair Road in 1947.

The exterior of the shrine is decorated with bright paintings of the Hindu gods Vishnu, Shiva and Ganesha, among others. The magnificent doors were salvaged in 1875 from a temple on the banks of the Umbilo River that was subsequently destroyed by floods. The temple's altar of sacrifice resembles an open lotus flower. The altar is not intended for ritual slaughter, but is, instead, the place where worshippers prostrate themselves before entering the temple in order to cleanse themselves of the three impurities: egoism, delusion and lust. Afterwards, it is said, 'angelic spirits go along with them'.

Shree Ambalavanaar Alayam Temple is one of Durban's many magnificent Hindu temples.

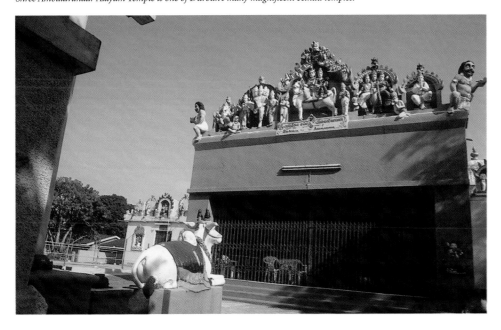

Beachwood mangroves

The beachwood mangroves on the northern banks of the Umgeni River are situated within a major urban residential centre. The site's unique indigenous vegetation includes Black Mangrove, Wild Cotton Tree, Lagoon Hibiscus, Bulrush and Limpopo Grass, all growing between high spring tide and mean sea level.

Following an uproar in 1985, after the government defence force decided to reopen a disused military shooting range in an area bordering the swamps, the city council declared the beachwood mangroves a national monument to protect not only their educational and historical value but also the lives of visitors. The swamp was declared a nature reserve, and extensive research was done towards rehabilitating the mangroves.

Visit the Beachwood Mangrove Nature Reserve

Although closed to the general public, special educational tours can be arranged through the reserve (031 205 1271).

Ohlange Institute (Inanda)

Large, straggly eucalyptus trees stand sentinel over the graves of Reverend John Langalibalele Dube and his wife on a shady hill at Ohlange Institute, overlooking the sprawling townships near Durban. The Institute, founded by Reverend Dube on a farm he bought in 1900, offered Africans quality education at a time when African education was neglected and undermined by the government.

John Dube was born in 1871. In 1903, on his return to South Africa after obtaining an Arts and Theology degree in the United States, he founded the *Ilanga Lase Natal* newspaper, which he ran and edited until 1934. He was frequently critical of the government of the time, which resulted in his arrest during the Bhambatha uprising of 1906.

Greatly impressed while in the United States, by the work of Booker T Washington, Reverend Dube established an industrial college for African boys in Inanda, based on the ideals of 'self-help and working hands'. He also founded an educational trust and built the Zulu Christian Industrial School, which later became famous as the Ohlange Institute. Generations of African

The Ohlange Institute is based on ideals of 'self-help and working hands' similar to those of Gandhi's Phoenix settlement, which lies only a kilometre away across the valley.

Reverend John Dube and his wife lie buried near their homestead at Ohlange Institute.

children were taught and encouraged at the Ohlange Institute.

In 1900, Reverend Dube founded the Natal Native Congress , which was later affiliated to the ANC. He became an advisor to the royal Zulu house under King Solomon kaDinuzulu, and was a member of the Native Representative Council. He was the first president (in 1912) of the ANC, a position from which he resigned in 1919 following disagreement within the ranks of the ANC on the issue of African volunteers in World War I.

A man of wisdom and foresight who spoke up for the Zulu people and fought for justice, John Dube was the author of five books in Zulu, including a novel set in the time of King Shaka; a biography of the prophet, Shembe; and a book instructing young people on good manners and behaviour. In 1936, his contribution to South

Africa and to African education was recognised when he became the first black African to be awarded an honorary doctorate of philosophy by the University of South Africa. He died in 1946.

Gandhi's Phoenix settlement

Mohandas Gandhi arrived in South Africa in 1893. Eleven years later, in 1904, he founded Phoenix, a small, non-racial settlement in Inanda, about 25 kilometres out of Durban, on about 32 hectares of what was then rural land.

Even though Gandhi did not spend much time at the settlement, especially after the Passive Resistance Campaign shifted to the Transvaal in 1906, it was here that he began to formulate his notion of *satyagraha*, or passive resistance, against the discriminatory laws of the government of the day. The inhabitants of Gandhi's ashram farmed and led a life based on the philosophy of *sarodaya*, or the ideal life, which Gandhi identified with self-sufficiency. He relocated a newspaper, *Indian Opinion*, to the ashram, where it was produced communally and printed.

Over time, informal townships sprang up around the city of Durban and engulfed the settlement. One of these was called Bhambayi – the Zulu version of the word 'Bombay' – referring to the Indian settlement nearby. Ironically, in the light of Gandhi's commitment to peace, Bhambayi became a hotbed of political violence during the 1980s.

In 1985, as part of the National Party's plan to consolidate the so-called homelands, about 900 Indian families were given notice to leave. Promises were made to compensate residents for buildings such as schools, houses and shops. Before the government could take action, however, Indian families living in the Phoenix settlement were attacked and their homes torched and looted, apparently by members of the surrounding African communities. After the riots, squatters moved into many of the ruined buildings.

The house Gandhi had lived in, his son's house, as well as the old printing press were ransacked and virtually destroyed in the violence. In 1988, the settlement was provisionally declared a national monument in an attempt to protect it until a solution could be found to the problems in the area. At the same time, plans were made to revitalise Gandhi's homestead by restoring parts of the settlement and establishing a museum and a park. Today, the park honours the memory of both Gandhi and John Dube, who lived nearby and wrote extensively about issues in the settlement. A well that Gandhi dug and built himself is situated in the park.

The Phoenix settlement has long been associated with the call for freedom in South Africa. From here came the first call for the release of Nelson Mandela and other political prisoners and, in 1971, the call to unban political parties and individuals. It was also from here that the Natal Indian Congress was revived on 2 October 1971. When the United Democratic Front was founded in 1983, it held its first national executive meeting at the settlement.

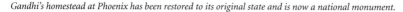

Gandhi's homestead at Phoenix has been restored to its original state and is now a national monument.

A little piece of India

After slavery was abolished in 1834, British settlers in Natal struck a deal with the Indian government to recruit indentured labour for their sugar, tea and coffee plantations. Thousands of poor Indians were enticed to South Africa with promises of attractive wages and repatriation after five years, or the right to settle in Natal as free men. The first indentured labourers reached Natal on 6 November 1860 and were soon followed by independent Indian traders. By 1865, there were about 5 300 Indians in Durban.

The original Indian settlers brought with them their food, language, dress and religions. A number of small, elaborately painted Hindu temples can be found in and around Durban where Hindu festivals such as Kavadi and Rhatha Yatra, where devotees walk on fire and nail beds and pierce their bodies, are held. The Riverside Soofie Mosque and Mausoleum are two of the holiest Muslim shrines in South Africa.

Ganesha Temple

The Ganesha Temple at Mount Edgecombe, just outside Durban, was built in 1899 by Kistappa Reddy, who came to South Africa in 1898 to work as an indentured labourer in the sugar-cane fields.

A thick plaster wall only 1.36 metres high surrounds the small temple. To the east is an entrance gate with deep mouldings and sculptures that take on a strong three-dimensional quality in the light. On either side of the entrance are representations of Ganesha. The whole enclosure and *sikhara* (tower) are lime-washed to complement the bright colours used elsewhere.

Riverside Soofie Mosque and Mausoleum

The original Riverside Soofie Mosque, established by Hazrath Saheb in 1895, was a simple octagonal building on a podium with a green, printed-steel roof. Due to earthworks on the neighbouring school grounds, part of the mosque developed cracks that required rebuilding. The new design was modelled on the old octagonal plan, but it was felt that an imposing dome, which has symbolic value, should cap the building. Inside, the mosque is expansive and spacious. The imam's residence, once situated near the mosque was demolished in 1968 under the Group Areas Act. In recent years, as the area has opened up and Muslim worshippers have returned to the suburb, a new residence has been built. Saheb is revered as a Muslim saint and many follow-ers visit his mausoleum, which is considered to be a place of healing.

In 1993, the mosque and the provincial heritage council were embroiled in a controversy after an 'entrepreneur' obtained a lease from the school adjacent to the mosque to use its sports fields as a golf driving-range. Flying balls damaged the windows of the mausoleum and it took many meetings, much diplomacy and finally the threat of legal action to close down the golfing range.

Juggernath Puri Temple

The 21-metre-high Juggernath Puri Temple near Tongaat is modelled on the famous temple of the same name on the banks of the Ganges River in India. It was built by Pandit Shiskishan Maharaj, a Hindu priest and Sanskrit scholar, who emigrated to South Africa in 1895 at the age of 24. He worked as an indentured labourer on the sugar-cane fields, saving his money to buy the land on which he built the temple over a period of five years. The sculptures are all his own work.

The building is unique in that Maharaj did not decorate every available surface of the *sikhara*, as in most temples. At one time, tall palms grew in the corners, with the *sikhara* in the centre. However, the palms have since been chopped down. On entering the dark temple, the image of Juggernath (the war-like god to whom the temple is dedicated) slowly becomes apparent in all his fearsome glory, complete with bright eyes, scary teeth and arms amputated in battle.

Mariannhill Monastery

When Catholic missionaries arrived in Durban, a group of traders with strong Protestant ties had already established themselves there. Struggling to find land in the central parts of the growing town, Catholic Trappist monks eventually stationed themselves in the hills surrounding Durban, from where they established many small missions in the province.

In *c.* 1885, Father Francis Pfanner, an Austrian monk, established a Trappist mission in a valley 'where the Mhlathuzane River flows in a long slow curve before disappearing into Durban harbour' near modern-day Pinetown. Mariannhill, as it was later named, thrived and, with a community of 285 monks, became the largest Trappist settlement in the world.

The buildings at Mariannhill were of such beauty that the brothers' European superiors regarded them as 'wasteful' in their loveliness. Self-reliance was one of the mission's main tenets, and even the stained glass for the church windows was made on the premises. The chapel is famous for its beautifully crafted wooden interior, and the elaborate St Joseph's Cathedral is, in form and adornment, a work of art.

The Valley of Monks, as Mariannhill was originally known, had a profound influence on

Mariannhill Monastery is famous for the beauty of its cloisters and elaborate chapels.

the development of those living in the area and on that of the province. The monks offered training in printing, bookbinding, tailoring, shoemaking, brickmaking, breadbaking, tanning, blacksmithing, carpentry and farming. To the disgust of many colonists, they opened St Francis College, the first non-racial school in the country.

By 1909, there were 49 Catholic missions throughout South Africa, the majority of which had been founded by the 'Mariannhillers'. Although some of the mission stations set up between the coast and the Drakensberg mountains by Trappist monks are easily visible from country roads, many are hidden deep in the grassy hills of the Midlands.

Visit Mariannhill

Mariannhill Monastery welcomes visitors of all religions. Listen to the monks chant in the background as you enjoy a warm drink at the Mariannhill Monastery Tea Garden (031 700 2706) before going on one of the walks organised in the mission grounds.

Kearsney: house, chapel and college

In 1905, plans were made to build a church in the hills outside Durban to serve the growing community around the farm Kearsney, which at the time was owned by J L Hulett, a lay preacher. Before this time, neighbours and family friends had worshipped at the family home and, later, in a small church nearby. A minister from the nearby farming district of Verulam made quarterly visits.

The outbreak of the Bhambatha uprising in 1906 delayed construction of the new church. The government claimed the farmhouse, then the home of the sugar baron, Sir Leige Hulett, as a military station. The church – complete with nave, chancel and vestry with a porch – was finished only in 1908. The red-brick, stucco building has something of an Old English appearance, with Gothic mouldings and tracery.

In 1921, Sir Leige Hulett donated his home to the Methodist Church as the foundation of Kearsney College. The college continued to operate from these premises until 1939, when it was moved to Botha's Hill. The chapel is now owned by the Hulett Corporation, which maintains the buildings and grounds. Nine of the original pews are still in the chapel.

Morewood Gardens: the first sugar mill

Edmund Morewood, an early British settler in Durban, is thought to be the founder of the sugar industry in Natal. A businessman and an astute politician, Morewood befriended the Voortrekkers and helped them negotiate with Zulu king Mpande. In return, the government of the Natalia Republic appointed him Durban's harbour-master and customs superintendent – a post he retained after the British annexed the region.

Morewood got the idea of planting sugar cane in Natal from the wild cane *umoba* he saw growing thickly near the coast. When the authorities granted him a farm between the Tongaat and the Umhlali Rivers (which he named 'Compensation' because he had wanted another farm), Morewood planted his first cane. It came from the island later known as Réunion. By 1852, he was growing three different types of cane on 42 hectares of land.

Morewood built his own sugar mill in 1851 and was able to exhibit his first processed sugar in 1852. Despite positive prospects, he could not raise the necessary capital to develop his project and ended up having to sell his estate. However, other farmers saw potential in his idea and by 1853 many were growing sugar.

Morewood's sugar mill was left to languish for a hundred years before it was discovered by the Hulett family. In 1948, a memorial garden with indigenous plants was established at the site to preserve what remained of Morewood's pioneering work. A pond was built on the location of the original millpond from which Morewood drew water for his factory, and a replica of the wooden mills used to crush juice from the sugar cane was erected. All that is left of Morewood's original buildings, however, is the foundation of crude, sun-dried bricks.

South of Durban

The first Europeans to explore the region south of Durban were traders. They encountered there the surviving members of tribes that had fled south in the aftermath of invasions by Zulu kings, Shaka and Dingane. In the valleys cut by numerous rivers, there was still wild game in abundance and evidence of Bushmen who hunted and gathered in the forests and grasslands.

In the far south between the Mzimkhulu and Mtamvuna rivers, was an area known as No Man's Land, sandwiched between the Zulu and Xhosa people. Annexed by the British colonial authorities in 1866 and named Alfred County after Prince Alfred, Queen Victoria's younger son, it became Natal's southernmost district.

Port Shepstone and surrounds

Following a trip to the mouth of the Mzimkhulu River, the surveyor-general of Natal decided to assess the river as a possible berthing point for ships, with an eye on developing the region. Land on either side of the river was reserved for settlement and by 1881 the area around the river had attracted many colonists, including some rather eccentric characters. Sugar and coffee was farmed and a limestone quarry opened. The surveyor-general's assessment led to the building of what soon became a thriving little harbour visited by small coasting ships. It was named Port Shepstone, after Sir Theophilus Shepstone.

Port Shepstone harbour

William Bazley, after whom Bazley Beach is named, played a key role in establishing the harbour at Port Shepstone on the Mzimkhulu River mouth. When Bazley was given the contract to build the harbour wall, he did all the underwater work himself, using homemade diving equipment. He was, apparently, harassed by sharks and, on one occasion, nearly drowned when a playful dog kept climbing onto his heavy underwater helmet each time he tried to surface.

The first ship to call at Port Shepstone was the *Somtseu*, in 1880. It was built in London and specially designed to manage the shallow harbours of Natal. For many years it plied its trade between Durban and Port Shepstone, calling at Port Shepstone every two weeks. The *Sandpiper* was Port Shepstone's first dredger and came into operation because ships were not able to enter the harbour during the dry winter months.

The old harbour wall, remnants of which can still be seen adjoining the fishing block down at the

The white Zulu chief

Henry Francis Fynn was one of the most intriguing and influential of the early settlers in southern KwaZulu-Natal. Not only was he a trader, writer, adventurer, philanthropist and colonial official, but by 1824 he had been made a Zulu *inkosi* (chief) after nursing King Shaka through an attempted assassination.

Shaka granted Fynn a large tract of land between the Tongaat and Mzimkhulu rivers. Realising he needed Shaka's protection, Fynn adopted many Zulu customs. Shaka even allowed him to take Zulu wives. After Shaka's assassination by Dingane, Fynn's position became less secure, and in 1831 his home was attacked and 40 people killed, among them some of his children.

While holding on to his position as a chief, Fynn became actively involved in colonial administration and held various positions in the colonial government from 1834 onwards. He established homesteads south of the Mtwalume River, working tirelessly for both the British and the Zulus. His efforts were not acknowledged by either: Zulu chiefs challenged his chiefdom and colonial officials did not recognise the legitimacy of his title to the land given him by Shaka. In later life, he married a white woman named Christina.

Henry Francis Fynn died of dysentery in 1861. His body was buried in Isipingo, just outside Durban, on a piece of land he once farmed. On his death, Duka, his son by one of his Zulu wives, succeeded him as chief. Duka's right to his chiefdom was also challenged, as was that of his son, Willie, and his grandson, Percy. The reign of the Fynns finally came to an end with Colin Fynn, whose title was successfully challenged by Bangibizo Luthuli.

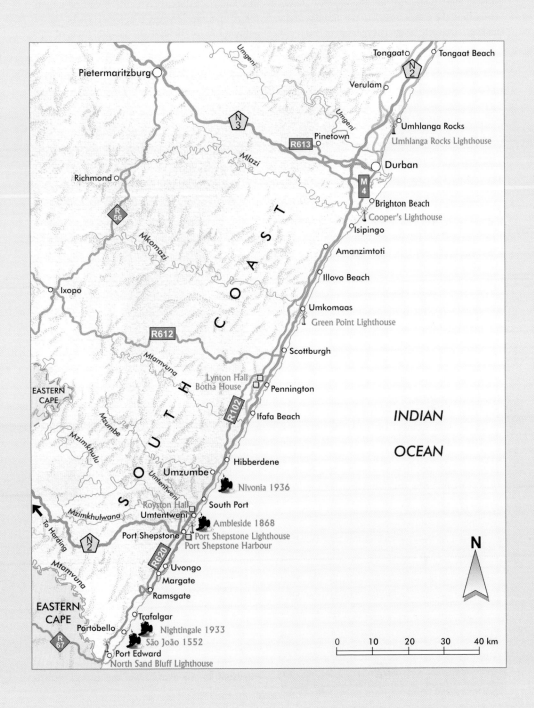

Pietermaritzburg

Tongaato   Tongaat Beach

N2

Verulam

Umngeni

N3

R613   Pinetown

Umngeni

Umhlanga Rocks
Umhlanga Rocks Lighthouse

Mlazi

Durban

Richmond

M4

Brighton Beach
Cooper's Lighthouse

R56

Isipingo

Mkomazi

Amanzimtoti

Illovo Beach

Ixopo

Umkomaas
Green Point Lighthouse

R612

Scottburgh

Mtamvuna

Lynton Hall
Botha House   Pennington

EASTERN
CAPE

R102

Ifafa Beach

Mzumbe

INDIAN

OCEAN

Mzimkhulu

Hibberdene

Umzumbe

Umtentweni

Nivonia 1936

Royston Hall
Mzimkhulwana   Umtentweni   South Port

Ambleside 1868

Port Shepstone
Port Shepstone Lighthouse
Port Shepstone Harbour

N2

to Harding

R620

Uvongo

Mtamvuna

Margate

Ramsgate

N

EASTERN
CAPE

Trafalgar

Portobello

Nightingale 1933
São João 1552

R67

Port Edward
North Sand Bluff Lighthouse

0   10   20   30   40 km

S O U T H   C O A S T

river mouth, was built of local rock. The stone was dowelled and clamped together and the centre of the wall filled with rubble. Engineer W Barnes Kinsey built the southern wall of the harbour in the late 1800s and early 1900s. The remains of this pretty wall can also be seen, as well as the quarry from which the stone for the earlier wall was mined.

The harbour became fully operational in 1893, and cargoes could be imported directly into Port Shepstone without having to be cleared by customs in Durban. In 1898, the customs house was built on the southern wharf but, sadly, had to be demolished when the new road was built some years later. Port Shepstone's harbour is no longer in use, having lost the battle against siltation and competition from the railway line from Durban. Port Shepstone, however, remains the transport and commercial capital of the south coast.

Umzumbe/Pumula village

The village of Umzumbe lies between Durban and Port Shepstone. Founded by American missionaries, the village is the place where crinoline dresses made their South African debut – one of its more dubious claims to fame. The dresses were worn by a newly married missionary, Laura Bridgman, prior even to the American Civil War.

Laura Bridgman and her husband, Reverend Henry Bridgman, arrived in Umzumbe to set up a mission on a site that had been located by Bridgman and another missionary, Reverend Elijah Robbins. Despite being attacked by wild hyenas on one of their first nights in Umzumbe, the Bridgmans and Robbins persisted with their mission work. Over time they befriended local chiefs and received permission to build schools and churches on tribal land. In 1873, the missionaries established a girls' boarding school, the Umzumbe Home for Kraal Girls. Three generations of Bridgmans gave a total of 279 years of service to god and country.

Royston Hall, Umtentweni

Royston Hall is magnificently situated on a promontory on the Mzimkhulu River near Port Shepstone. It is the oldest residence in the area and was occupied from 1906 to 1942 by Brigadier-General John Robinson Royston aka 'Galloping Jack', a prominent figure at the time. Royston's wife was murdered in the house in 1959.

The house was originally known as Kingston and later as Mount Romani. It was severely damaged by fire in 1986 and the top floor had to be replaced. A small flat was built over the original water tank, which is now used as a cellar, and the stables were converted into servants' quarters. The railway passes near the north side of the house.

Lynton Hall and Botha House

A beautiful long road winds through the coastal forest of Pennington to the wrought-iron gates of Lynton Hall, once the residence of one of Natal's foremost sugar barons, Frank Reynolds. Lynton Hall was commissioned in 1884 by Charles Reynolds and was designed by the famous architects, Street Wilson and Fyfe. (Street Wilson also designed the Pietermaritzburg Railway Station, now a national monument.) Reynolds' brother, Sir Frank Reynolds, acquired the house in 1919 and hosted many dignitaries there, including General Jan Smuts, the Earl of Athlone and Princess Alice, sister of King George V. Among the famous writers who stayed at the Writer's Cottage on the estate were Roy Campbell, Edward Rowarth, Noel Langley, Sir Percy Fitzpatick and Sir Laurens van der Post.

A close friend of Prime Minister Louis Botha, Sir Frank built a beach house for the prime minister in 1920 on the northeast boundary of his estate. Botha died before it was completed, but his wife lived there until her death. Now known as Botha House, the gabled building was entrusted to the nation for the use of future prime ministers.

Visit Umzumbe

A seaside village, Umzumbe offers splendid accommodation at the Pumula Beach Hotel (039 684 6717), a family-run business right on the shores of the Indian Ocean. The Pumula, as the hotel is known, is a familiar landmark and worth a visit, if only to peer at the stories pinned to the walls of the pub. There is even a photograph of the last leopard, which was killed in the Umzumbe district in 1921.

A tale of two brothers

The Reynolds family is just one of the many that settled along the sugar-cane belt of Natal in the late 1800s. The family's South African history begins with the arrival in 1852 from Devonshire of the two Reynolds brothers, Thomas and Lewis. They took up farming and milling sugar at Umhlali, on the north coast, and when a run-down sugar mill at Umzinto on the south coast came up for sale in 1873, Lewis bought it. His two sons, Frank and Charles, took over the running of both the mill and the estate, with some success.

Charles Reynolds so mistreated the Indian indentured labourers who worked his sugar estates that the Natal colonial government threatened to cease all further allotments of indentured labour to the estate. He was eventually removed from the management of the estate and left the country in some disgrace. He died, supposedly after he was stabbed by a jealous husband in South America, and his body was pickled in rum, placed in a lead coffin and brought back to Umzinto to be buried in the churchyard at Lynton Hall.

A quite different character from his brother, Frank Reynolds was knighted in 1916 and bought Lynton Hall from Umzinto Sugar Mill at Sezela in 1919. He extended Lynton Hall and had the gardens laid out on part of the 65-hectare estate. A member of Durban's A-list of families, who served on the Natal Legislative Council, he enjoyed a few special privileges, one of which was his choice of rare plants imported from Kew Gardens in London by Durban's Botanical Gardens. He left a heritage garden that boasts one of the finest private collections of exotic species in Africa, as well as a number of magnificent indigenous plants.

Sir Frank Reynolds died in 1930, a year after he held a funeral for his leg, which had been amputated. Lynton Hall passed to his son, Lewis, who was General Smuts's private secretary and a member of parliament for the south coast.

Visit Lynton Hall

Lynton Hall (033 263 2713) is still under the ownership of the Reynolds family and is now a beautiful boutique hotel with nine luxurious rooms. The Umdoni Park golf course is nearby.

Wrecks off the south coast

More than 40 ships have sunk in the treacherous waters south of Durban. The remains of one, the *Nightingale*, are still visible on the beach; others are remembered by structures built from their timbers, and some have given their names to places near where they sank. Yet others live on in the pages of books.

São João (1552)

On 11 June 1552, the Portuguese East Indiaman *São João*, captained by Manuel de Sousa Sepulvida, ran aground during a storm along the south coast while en route to Europe from the Indian port of Cochin. The vessel was heavily overloaded, as was common at a time when European shipowners were importing as much as they could as cheaply as possible. Heavily pounded by the sea, it started breaking up just north of the Mtamvuna River near modern-day Port Edward, and was finally driven by raging wind and waves onto the shore where it smashed to pieces against the rocks. More than 100 of the 200 Portuguese and 400 slaves on board drowned.

On 7 July 1552, after camping for 12 days at the site of the wreck, a procession of survivors led by the captain set off in search of Delagoa Bay (Maputo), which at the time was visited periodically by Portuguese ships. The journey took three months and the travellers suffered terrible hardship, living off the land when food ran out and fending off hostile tribesmen along the way.

Reduced to about 120 persons, the party finally arrived in Delagoa Bay but the captain, by this time delirious with hunger and exhaustion, refused to believe it was their destination and insisted on pressing on. Across the river mouth,

Pounded by the sea, all that is left of the 1933 wreck of the Nightingale *are rusted bits of metal on the rocks at Glenmore Beach.*

they were attacked by hostile tribesmen who stole all they had, including their clothes. The captain, his wife and two children died shortly afterwards. The few survivors – three women slaves, fourteen male slaves and eight Portuguese – were rescued by boat and taken to the Port of Mozambique.

Ambleside (1868)
On 30 August 1868, the 535-ton British barque *Ambleside* was returning to Liverpool from Karachi with a cargo of 2 850 bales of cotton and linseed when it ran into a storm and was wrecked on the rocks between the Mzimkhulu and the Mtentweni rivers, north of Port Shepstone.

Witnesses to the disaster alerted a recent settler named Archibald Sinclair, who rushed to the scene to find that the crew had made it to shore safely. Even the captain's dog was on dry land. (Doris Webster, Sinclair's granddaughter, still has a letter from Captain Robert Bowie in London thanking Sinclair for his help and mentioning that his dog had recovered.) Much of the ship's cotton cargo was salvaged or auctioned

on the spot, after which the survivors made their weary way to Durban over rough terrain and through the many rivers. One of Sinclair's daughters, Kate Tinney, recalls that her mother owned a mattress stuffed with the 'wool' – actually cotton – given to her by the captain.

Sinclair salvaged timber from the wreck and used it in his house, naming his farm Ambleside in honour of the barque. Today, a number of bed-and-breakfasts, roads and homes in the region also carry the name, and many Port Shepstone locals own relics from the ship.

Nightingale (1933)
In 1933, the *Nightingale*, a 150-ton vessel belonging to fishing giant Irvin and Johnson, ran into trouble off Munster, near Port Edward. The weather, which had been fine when the ship left Durban, deteriorated as the afternoon wore on. By midnight, the *Nightingale* was dangerously close to shore at Glenmore Beach. It struck a rock and a sailor was washed overboard. Fortunately, he managed to swim to shore in front of the police

Candle power

Fourteen lighthouses stand sentry over the southern KwaZulu-Natal coastline, of which three are of historical significance. The lighthouses at Port Shepstone and Port Edward are open to the public.

Old Bluff Lighthouse

The Old Bluff Lighthouse was commissioned in 1867 and was for many years the only one on the east coast of Africa. Sadly, it was demolished in 1940 and replaced by Cooper's Lighthouse near Brighton Beach in the south and Umhlanga Rocks Lighthouse in the north.

Port Shepstone Lighthouse

The Port Shepstone Lighthouse is one of the two oldest functioning lighthouses on the KwaZulu-Natal coast, having been in service since it was commissioned in 1892. It was completed in 1895 and was replaced by an unusual cast-iron structure in 1905. The lighthouse was originally commissioned for Scottburgh, but was relocated to the bluff at Port Shepstone as it was too small to warn ships of the dangerous Aliwal Shoal – a shallow reef fairly close to land.

Green Point Lighthouse

Not to be confused with the lighthouse of the same name in Cape Town, KwaZulu-Natal's Green Point Lighthouse is located at Clanstal, near Umkomaas, on the south coast. It is a familiar landmark on the drive between Umkomaas and Scottburgh.

Built in 1905, the lighthouse was automated in 1961 and powered by electricity instead of petroleum vapour. It flashes two white lights every 15 seconds to accompany its red subsidiary light, warning ships of the dangers of the Aliwal Shoal.

North Sand Bluff Lighthouse

The southernmost lighthouse in KwaZulu-Natal, the North Sand Bluff Lighthouse in Port Edward, was commissioned in 1968 and rebuilt in 1999. Surrounded by subtropical vegetation with stunning sea views, it is situated in one of the most beautiful spots along this stretch of coast.

station at Marina Beach, some way up the coast. By daybreak, strong seas had lifted the ship onto the rocks, making it easier to help the rest of the 11-strong crew to shore with ropes and ladders.

The cargo of fish was sold to bystanders, who preserved their purchases by burying them in the sand, layered with blocks of ice. As for the rest of the wreck, a Glenmore local named John Henry Velkoop bought it, sold the coal in its hull and loaded all the salvageable parts – brass, timber, vents and mast – onto his ox wagon. He carted the whole lot up the hill to his home, where he planted the mast in his garden so that he could watch the annual sardine run from the crow's nest.

The hull of the *Nightingale* remained almost intact for the next 25 years. These days, however, all you can see at low tide are the boiler and some metal parts. The propeller and rudder are on display on the front lawn at Kinderstrand, a children's holiday home at Glenmore Beach.

Nivonia (1936)

During a blustery night in July 1936, a Durban-based whale-catching vessel, the *Nivonia*, ran ashore at Pumula, then known as Melbourne Bay. Through enormous waves, the captain managed to fire a harpoon to shore and the Norwegian crew were able to climb down the attached Manila rope to safety.

There to help them was Garnet Blamey who, having seen distress rockets from his home some way up the Injambili River, had rowed down the torrential river in his small boat. The boat overturned under the old railway bridge, but Blamey swam ashore and – barely escaping decapitation by the harpoon – was able to assist the distressed sailors.

Pietermaritzburg and Midlands

Red-brick Victorian buildings and a strong association with the Imperial military may fool one into thinking that Pietermaritzburg was founded by the British. In fact, the foundations for Pietermaritzburg were laid along the Umsinduzi River and the smaller Dorpspruit stream by Dutch-speaking Voortrekkers. Disenchanted with the British authorities in the Cape, they had packed their belongings and headed north through what is now the Free State and over the Drakensberg into Natal.

The Voortrekker presence in Natal was perceived by the governor of the Cape Colony, Sir George Napier, both as an encroachment on Zulu territory and a threat to the 'independence' of Port Natal (Durban). Conflict between British and Boer continued along with conflict between the Boers and the Zulu under the leadership of Dingane, culminating in the Battle of Ncome/Blood River. After the British annexation of Natal in 1843, most of the Voortrekkers who had settled in Natal inspanned their oxen and trekked back to the Highveld north of the Vaal River.

Places of historical importance in Pietermaritzburg and the surrounding area carry one far back in time as well as to the more recent past. The lush countryside has a rich natural as well as a political and social heritage. It was at Howick in the Midlands that Nelson Mandela was captured and it was in Pietermaritzburg that Mahatma Gandhi was forcibly removed from a train, an experience he called one of the most significant in his life.

The Natal Botanical Gardens in Pietermaritzburg were once considered 'the finest seedling-producing institution in the British Empire'.

Pietermaritzburg: redbrick and resistance

After it was taken over by the British in 1843, Pietermaritzburg became a busy stopover for settlers, traders and military personnel moving between Port Natal (Durban) and the hinterland. The 45th Regiment was stationed at Fort Napier on a hill in an outlying area of the city for 15 years, still a record for length of overseas service in the British army.

There is much debate about the origins of the city's name and some contemporary historians dispute the widely held belief that it stems from the names of two Voortrekker leaders, Piet Retief and Gert Maritz. It appears that any authoritative record of the town's naming has been lost, possibly in the conflict that arose in the 1830s between the Boers and the independent kingdom of Zululand.

Although it has always been considered a sleepy hollow, serving as a centre for the surrounding agricultural industry, Pietermaritzburg has in recent decades become the capital and administrative hub of the province.

City centre

Pietermaritzburg is known for its Victorian buildings, which were constructed in the course of the 19th century to meet the needs of the growing town: libraries, hospitals, museums, theatres, banks, hotels, railway stations, schools, churches and the many administrative structures that serve as a reminder of the past.

World's View

At the Umgeni River, Voortrekker leader Piet Retief and his party cut a route from the river along the ridge of hills behind where the Cedara Agricultural School now stands to the knoll up in the modern-day suburb of Hilton. Two old wagon tracks are still clearly visible here: one goes down the hill to Edendale, and the other passes World's View with a commanding view of the city. It is possible that the wagons went down World's View and, because the alternative route was less steep, came up the Edendale track. The section at World's View is well preserved and can be authenticated from original documents. The site has a lovely garden from which you can see a section of the old wagon track before it disappears into the forest. Lower down, the path of the old road can be seen clearly, as can marks made by wagon wheels and brake shoes on the rocks.

A small wall bears a brass plaque that reads:

'The road winding below along the ridge to Pietermaritzburg was used by the Voortrekkers who crossed the Drakensberg into Natal in 1838 and for many years afterwards continued to be used as the main road from Port Natal into the interior by the early pioneers and transport riders.'

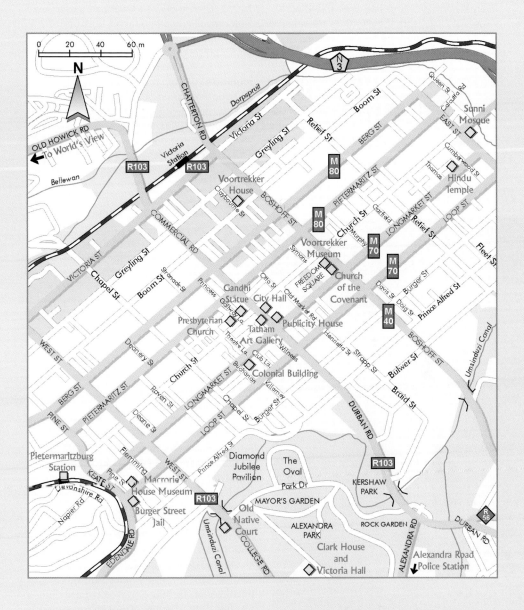

0   20   40   60. m

N

OLD HOWICK RD
To World's View

Bellewan

CHATTERTON RD

Dorpspruit

Victoria St

Victoria Station

R103   R103

COMMERCIAL RD

VICTORIA ST

Greyling St

Chapel St

WEST ST

BERG ST

PIETERMARITZ ST

PINE ST

Pietermaritzburg Station

Devonshire Rd

Napier Rd

KEATE ST

Flemming St

Pine St

Greyling St

Boom St

Stanock St

Princess

Deanery St

Church St

Raven St

Deane St

Prince Alfred St

EDENDALE RD

Umsinduzi Canal

COLLEGE RD

Claybourne St

Voortrekker House

BOSHOFF ST

Gandhi Statue

Gallwey St

Symons

Otto St

Old Market Rd

FREEDOM SQUARE

Presbyterian Church

City Hall

Tatham Art Gallery

Theatre La.   Club La.

Buchanan

LONGMARKET ST

LOOP ST

Chapel St

Burger St

Killarney

Witness

Publicity House

Colonial Building

WEST ST

Prince Alfred St

Macrorie House Museum

Burger Street Jail

R103

Diamond Jubilee Pavilion

Old Native Court

The Oval

Park Dr

MAYOR'S GARDEN

ALEXANDRA PARK

Clark House and Victoria Hall

Greyling St

Retief St

Boom St

BERG ST

M 80

PIETERMARITZ ST

Voortrekker Museum

M 80

Church St
Murphy

Garfield

LONGMARKET ST

M 70

Church of the Covenant

M 70

Davis St   Burger St

Dog St

M 40

Henrietta St   Strapp St

DURBAN RD

Queen St   Colamba Rd

EAST ST

Cumberwood St

Thomas

Sunni Mosque

Retief St

LOOP ST

Fleet St

Hindu Temple

Prince Alfred St

BOSHOFF ST

Bulwer St

Braid St

R103

KERSHAW PARK

ROCK GARDEN

DURBAN RD

ALEXANDRA RD

R56

Alexandra Road Police Station

Umsinduzi Canal

City Hall

Recognised by 'Ripley's Believe It or Not' as the largest red-brick structure south of the equator, the magnificent structure housing the City Hall at the corner of Church and Commercial streets is easily Pietermaritzburg's best-known landmark.

By the 1880s, with the growth of the colonial settlement, the need for a new town hall had become urgent. In 1884, the old town hall was demolished to make way for a new building on the site of the old *raadsaal* (meeting place) of the Volksraad of the short-lived Boer republic of Natalia. On 5 February 1891, the foundation stone of the old town hall, laid in 1860 by Prince Alfred, was re-laid at the site by Sir Charles Mitchell.

The City Hall's red-brick clock tower is a familiar sight in Pietermaritzburg.

The new building's main hall was 35 metres long with a 16-metre proscenium framing a vast organ with decorated pipes – the biggest pipe organ in the southern hemisphere. The organ had cost the citizens of Pietermaritzburg the sum of £6 737. There was also a lesser hall, a courtroom with council's chambers for the legislative assembly or upper house and ample accommodation for the offices of the growing municipality.

Five years after the completion of this municipal palace, it was razed by fire. The building that was erected in its place on the same site was designed in Flemish Renaissance style, right up to the clock tower.

Publicity House

The building known as Publicity House was erected in 1884 on the site of the original Voortrekker jail to house the colonial borough police. Soon thereafter, a fire department, complete with horse-drawn fire-fighting units, was established at the rear of the building. The building is located next to the City Hall which, ironically, burned down in 1898.

During the apartheid years, a bell in the tower of the building was used to ring the nine o'clock curfew, after which all black people had to be off the city streets. Today, this classic red-brick building houses Pietermaritzburg's Publicity Association and has a much friendlier face.

Presbyterian Church

One of the first British churches to be established in the settlement was the Presbyterian Church in Church Street. It was built on land donated by the Natal government on condition that a clock be installed in the church tower. The foundation stone was laid in 1852 and the building completed two years later – without a clock. Twenty-three years down the line, a clock and bell were installed in the tower, making it Pietermaritzburg's only public timepiece until 1893.

During the Anglo-Zulu War of 1879 the church, like so many other sturdy colonial buildings of the time, was converted into a fortified place of refuge, although never used as such. In 1883, the building was extended to the rear, giving it its characteristic T-shape. The architecture of the church tower is Victorian

Gothic Revival, typical of Presbyterian churches of the time.

The church's clock and bell were sold to the Greytown Queen's Diamond Jubilee Committee. The clock served as Greytown's town hall clock until – thought to be beyond repair – it was taken down and stored in a basement and replaced with a modern electric clock. In 1977, hearing of the clock's fate, church authorities approached the Greytown municipality and brought the old clock back to Pietermaritzburg, where it was repaired and installed in its original location in the clock tower.

Minor alterations were made to the old church when it was sold to the government in 1942 for use by government officials. However, the main structure, currently used as a centre for the arts, remains unchanged.

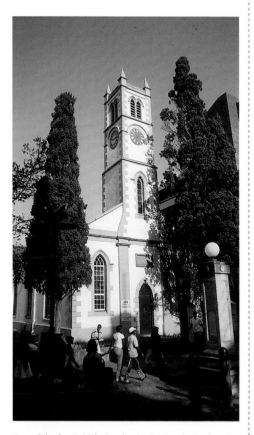

One of the first British churches in the city, the Presbyterian Church is now a centre for the arts.

Colonial Building, Umgeni Magistrates' Court

The Colonial Building on Church Street, opposite the Presbyterian Church, is one of the city's most significant landmarks. It is part of a complex that included the old Native High Court, and was built on a site purchased by the colonial administration in 1865. Before it became the Umgeni Magistrates' Court (when the High Court moved to new premises in College Road), the building contained the offices of the Secretary for Native Affairs, Sir Theophilus Shepstone.

In its day, the Colonial Building housed the administrative arms of the legislature of the Colony of Natal and also the deeds office. The three-storey building extends about 22 metres down Galway Lane, at which point it becomes a two-storey structure enclosing four courtyards. It was designed in late Roman classic style and was completed in 1902. After the dissolution of the colonial administration in 1910, the state-owned building was used for a variety of purposes. It has mostly been left unoccupied for the past two decades but is scheduled for renovation, whereafter it will house the offices of the Master of the Supreme Court.

The Colonial Building is an architectural gem that is scheduled for renovation.

Voortrekkers in Pietermaritzburg

The most important reminders of Voortrekker presence in Pietermaritzburg are contained in the Voortrekker House Museum Complex on the corner of Church and Boshoff streets. The Church of the Covenant and a small thatch-roofed cottage next to it that once belonged to the Boer leader Andries Pretorius are the main sites at the complex. The cottage has been restored and is open to the public.

The complex includes the Longmarket Street Girls' School, erected between 1905 and 1910, the first girls' school in the growing settlement. Newly renovated, the building is of architectural interest and houses a number of exhibitions relating to Pietermaritzburg's development.

Church of the Covenant

The small Church of the Covenant, or Church of the Vow (bottom left) as it is sometimes called, was erected in 1840. The church, typically Cape Dutch in style, was built to commemorate a decisive battle against the Zulu, the Battle of Ncome/Blood River. The name derives from the vow made on 9 December 1838 by Andries Pretorius that should God grant the Boers victory they would build a church. A Voortrekker *wenkommando* – literally, 'victorious commando' – achieved that victory on 16 December 1838 without suffering any losses. Apart from its historical importance, the Church of the Covenant is of immense cultural significance to many Afrikaans-speaking South Africans.

Over the years, the church has been used as a school, blacksmith's shop, mineral water factory, chemist's shop and tearoom before ownership was finally recovered by the Church Council in 1910. The church was subsequently declared a national monument.

A variety of artefacts are housed in the church, including an old wagon, flintlock rifles, Piet Retief's prayer book and the original neo-Gothic pulpit, an octagonal structure four metres in height that is made of local hardwood. It consists of a plinth, lectern and canopy and was crafted in 1840, the year the church was built. The pulpit has been accorded the status of a national cultural treasure.

Voortrekker House

On 8 April 1846, six years after the Church of the Vow was built, an erf on 33 Boom Street was granted to Petrus Gerhardus Pretorius. It is believed, however, that the house on the plot of land was built a little earlier, making it the oldest building in Pietermaritzburg and the only surviving house built by a Voortrekker. The small double-storey structure (bottom right) is built of local shale with a front façade of four 12-paned casement windows and a thatched roof.

Once the Supreme Court, this stately building now houses the Tatham Art Gallery's collection.

The Umgeni Magistrates' Court, with its traditional red-brick walls, corrugated-iron roof and a verandah, dates back to around 1873. The building was completed under the supervision of the civil engineer for Natal, Major Antony Durnford, a well-known figure at the time who was killed at the battle of Isandlwana in 1879. One of the first balls given by the governor of Natal, Sir Garnet Wolseley, was held in its hall, which was once the largest in Pietermaritzburg. The building now serves as a court dealing with sexual offences.

Tatham Art Gallery (Old Supreme Court)

The original Supreme Court building was erected in 1871 opposite the Volksraad building (which was demolished when the City Hall was built). The Supreme Court building is now the Tatham Art Gallery. The Court and various government departments were housed there over the years and it was once the hub of administrative life in Pietermaritzburg. At the time of the Anglo-Zulu War of 1879, the central safe area of the city was constructed around the building, entrenching it

further as the centre of activity in Pietermaritzburg. Electric lights were installed in 1894 and additions made to the building in 1898.

In the adjacent gardens are several monuments that reflect the history of the city: a memorial arch erected in honour of those who served their country during the two World Wars; a striking monument to those who died in the Anglo-Zulu

British soldiers stand in stony silence in the gardens adjacent to the Tatham Art Gallery.

War of 1879; and a memorial dedicated to colonists who died in the South African War (1899–1902).

Cloete's Cannon, which was cast in Scotland in 1812 and brought to Natal in 1842 by Colonel Josias Cloete, stands in front of the Anglo-Zulu War monument. In the days when the Supreme Court building housed the post office, this cannon would be fired to let everyone know the mail had arrived from Durban.

Old Native Court, College Road

Throughout the 150 years of its existence, Pietermaritzburg has been the capital of Natal's legal administration and the history of the Native Court is inextricably linked to that of the legal system. The building that was constructed in the 1880s to house the Native Court was located in College Road, outside the central business district and away from white suburban areas. It was, at the same time, relatively close to Burger Street Jail. The Native Court was finally abolished in the 1950s.

The building, a typical example of late 1800s architecture, was also used for the administration of customary law in the Colony. It served for a time as Pietermaritzburg's Supreme Court and, during the apartheid era, was the scene of many high-profile trials. The first of these was the trial in 1979 of 24-year old James Daniel Mange who was accused of planning 'the extermination of the magistrate and police sergeant at Whittlesea near Queenstown'. Mange was sentenced to death at the College Road Supreme Court (as it was by

Park life

The area now known as Alexandra Park has been used as a recreational area since the first British occupation of Pietermaritzburg in 1843. The Umsinduzi River, which meanders through the park, was popular for swimming parties, and leafy trees created the ideal setting for picnics and late-afternoon strolls.

The park's Diamond Jubilee Pavilion, was built to celebrate Queen Victoria's 60th year on the throne. This traditional Victorian red-brick structure with cast-iron work is the centrepiece of the park's oval, the domain of cricket in the city for many years and of military bands in the Colony of Natal. A few old wrought-iron Victorian lampposts are still dotted around the oval.

Another Victorian cast-iron structure, the bandstand under the trees near the Pavilion, has hosted many military bands over the years and was once a popular spot for cream teas. The park is a unique combination of open and traditional recreational spaces and includes stone footbridges from the settler era, the Macfarlane Bridge and the O'Brien Bridge.

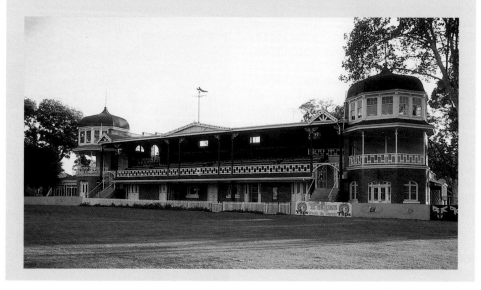

then known) and 11 of his co-accused were given sentences of between 13 and 18 years. The conflict that raged outside the court after the trial was, apparently, the first time South Africans engaged the police in armed combat.

For his part, Mange survived to become the leader of the Soccer Party in South Africa's first democratic elections in 1994.

Another well-publicised trial that took place in the building, in 1982, was that of Major 'Mad' Mike Hoare who, together with his men, had hijacked an Air India aeroplane to return to South Africa after a failed coup attempt in the Seychelles. In 1983, the courthouse was bombed by the ANC, with no loss of life.

Alexandra Road Police Station

The Alexandra Road Police Station was built in 1891 for use by the Natal Mounted Police, later the Natal Police, who played an active role in the South African War of 1899 and in suppressing the Bhambatha uprising of 1906. Members of the force fought alongside British troops in the Anglo-Zulu War of 1879, 33 of them dying at the Battle of Isandlwana. By 1906, the Natal Mounted Police numbered about 13 000 men.

Typical of Pietermaritzburg's red-brick buildings, the double-storey, U-shaped station has an attractive front archway and a roof of orange Broseley tiles, which were once common but are now almost unobtainable. When the station was first built, it had a guardroom, numerous offices, a quartermaster's store, stables, a forage room, an officer's lounge and a mess hall. The mess hall, kitchen and a hall are housed in separate, single-storey buildings. The stables and storerooms were later converted into garages, flats and offices, all of which are in use today. In front of the building are two muzzle-loading cannons that were originally used to guard Fort Napier.

Prior to the completion of their barracks at the Alexandra Police Station, the Natal Mounted Police shared premises with other police units in what is now Publicity House. In 1921, the Alexandra Road Barracks were taken over by the South African Police, into which the Natal Police had by then been incorporated.

Macrorie House Museum

Macrorie House was built around 1860 in a once affluent area at the top of Loop Street. It was purchased ten years later by Bishop William Kenneth and Agnes Macrorie who lived there in some style for over 20 years. Now a museum and an important part of the city's heritage, the house was lovingly restored in the 1970s. Like many old

Macrorie House Museum offers a glimpse of a vanished way of life.

Alan Paton's old school

Russell High School opened in Chapel Street in 1873 when, although known as the Girls' Model School, it had 53 boys as pupils as well as 116 girls and seven teachers. Parts of the original building were demolished in 1905–6 and six classrooms and a room for a cooking class were built. By 1910, there were 600 girls at the school. New premises were found in Berg Street and the name of the school was changed to Berg Street Government School and, in 1941, to Russell High School (after Robert Russell, the superintendent of education). The primary school was separated and moved to other premises.

The school, which counts author Alan Paton (author of *Cry, the Beloved Country*) among its alumni, is strongly associated with the development of education in KwaZulu-Natal. The building is architecturally pleasing with its red-brick longitudinal form and roof of Broseley tiles, bargeboards and lovely sash windows.

buildings, it has its share of ghost stories, and rattling chains and screams have been heard coming from beneath the floor boards. The 'lady in black', possibly a nun, has been sighted in the chapel and is the cause of much puzzlement because no nun ever lived or died in the house.

The museum is well worth a visit. Many of its furnishings, such as the Blüthner baby grand piano, have been donated by local residents.

Clark House and Victoria Hall

Clark House, named in honour of R D Clark, the school's headmaster between 1879 and 1902, stands in the grounds of Maritzburg College in College Road. It is one of the best-known school buildings in South Africa. Built in neo-Gothic style, it is considered by many to be architecturally unique despite the alterations that have been made to the back of the building in recent years.

Clarke House and Victoria Hall are some of the best-known school buildings in South Africa.

Pietermaritzburg Railway Station is famous both for its architecture and as the place where Mohandas Gandhi was kicked off a train.

The school building was erected in 1887 and the adjoining Victoria Hall ten years later. During the South African War of 1899–1902, Clarke House was evacuated and, with Victoria Hall, was used as a hospital for British troops.

Pietermaritzburg Railway Station

The original railway line between Durban and Pietermaritzburg was completed in November 1880. The first station, a simple wood-and-iron structure, was replaced in 1892 by Pietermaritzburg Railway Station, a red-brick structure designed by the well-known architect, W Street-Wilson. Of particular interest is the cast-steel roof structure – the first of its kind and size to be manufactured locally – as well as the Oregon pine ceilings, staircase, banisters, and doors and windows.

While the Pietermaritzburg Railway Station building is something of a showpiece, it is better known as the place where the young Mohandas Gandhi was kicked off a train for sitting in a 'Whites Only' carriage. A statue of Gandhi stands in the pedestrian walkway leading from the station towards City Hall.

Burger Street Jail

The Voortrekker prison, located on the town's Market Square, was replaced in 1862 by the Burger Street Jail, which was built away from the town centre on the road to Fort Napier. In its early days, the jail housed prisoners of both sexes and included a death row. Initially, each block had its own gallows. H-block's gallows (which were apparently never used) stretched from one wall to another above trapdoors; E-block's are still standing and consist of a plank sticking out of an upper-storey door from where condemned prisoners could be hanged in public.

In 1879, following news of the unexpected defeat of the British army by the Zulu at Isandlwana, hasty arrangements were made to incarcerate the governor and his staff at the prison for their protection. In more normal circumstances, the building was used as a medium-security prison, chiefly housing prisoners who had not been sentenced, although maximum-security prisoners were also held there occasionally.

Chief Langalibalele Hlubi was imprisoned at the Burger Street Jail in 1873, as was King Dinuzulu after the Bhambatha uprising of 1906. More recently, the cells held prominent ANC leaders Harry Gwala and Archie Gumede, as well as members of the Natal Indian Congress, Omar Essack, A S Chetty, S B Mongal and Mike Motala. Rumours that Nelson Mandela was held here overnight are untrue.

The jail was closed in 1989. Today, it houses Project Gateway, a Christian self-help project. Tours of the prison blocks of old are permitted.

Burger Street Jail's notorious E Block where hangings took place.

Pietermaritzburg's mosque and temples

Long before Gandhi's unscheduled stop at Pietermaritzburg station in 1893, many Indian indentured labourers had completed their terms of indenture at the coast and were moving inland. Temples and other religious structures are a testament to their presence.

Sunni mosque

This mosque (bottom left), built in 1903, was popularly known as the 'Top Mosque' since it was situated at the 'top' end of Church Street. Another mosque, known as 'Middle Mosque', was built in 1942 at the lower end of Church Street. Construction of the first mosque was funded by a successful Pietermaritzburg trader, Mr Bayat, who was one of the founders of the Natal Indian Congress and in whose house Gandhi stayed after the famous train episode of 1893. In 1901, Bayat imported a group of craftsmen from India to build new premises for his retail business. The result, Bayat's Building, was an architectural landmark for more than 70 years.

Satya Vardhak Sabha Crematorium and Waiting Room

When Hindu Indians arrived in Natal in the 1860s, they brought with them the practice of cremation. In the late 19th century, an open-air cremation platform was built, the ruins of which can still be seen in an outlying area of Pietermaritzburg along the Old Greytown Road. Among the more unusual monuments in the country, the crematorium and cemetery stand on ground that has been used as a burial site for over a century.

In the late 1920s, Satya Vardhak Sabha, an organisation that taught the Vedic philosophy of reincarnation, built a small vernacular waiting room for mourners and a new cremation chamber on the site of the old open-air crematorium. The waiting room, of classical pavilion design, was joined to the crematorium by a canopy (bottom right). The cremation chamber itself was a large, square chamber, with steel fire doors, where the funeral pyre was lit. It was replaced in 1954 by a modern gas crematorium that was built behind the existing building by the Satya Vardhak Sabha and the Veda Dharma Sabha, another Hindu organisation with which it had merged in 1940.

Hindu temple

The Sri Siva Soobramoniar and Marriamen Temple in Longmarket Street, built in 1898, is the oldest complex of its kind in Pietermaritzburg and a national monument. It is the venue for a Firewalking Festival in which devotees walk barefoot across a pit of smoking coals (on Good Friday) after a ten-day fast.

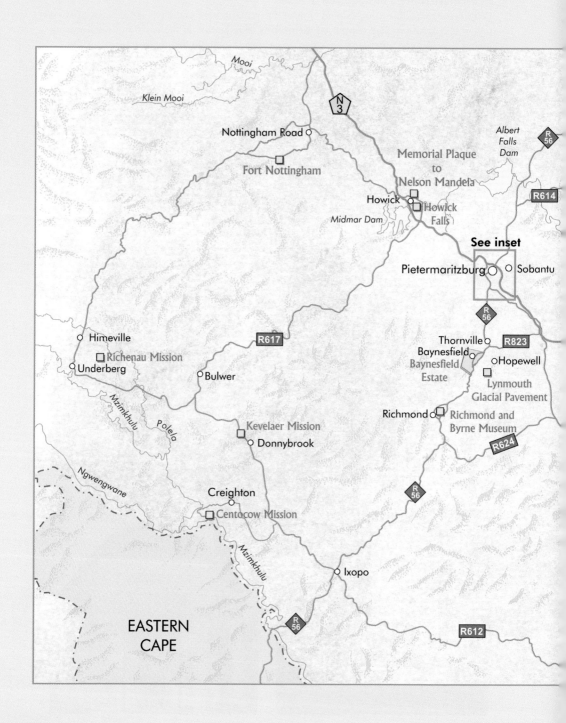

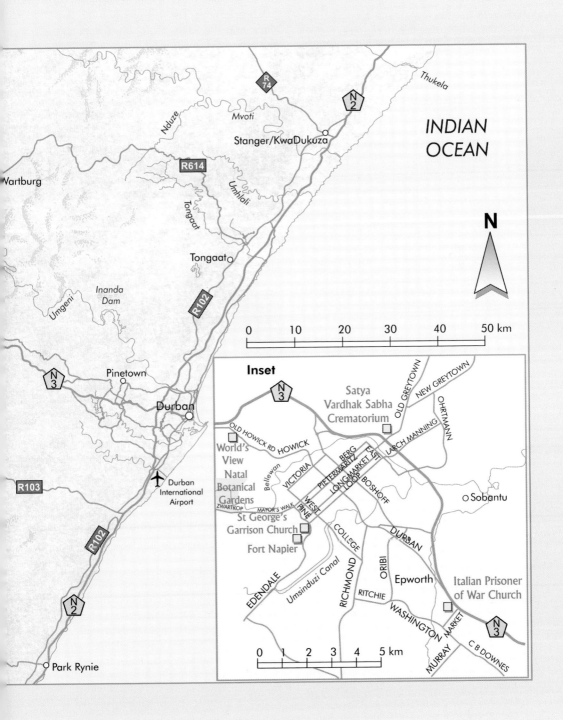

INDIAN
OCEAN

N

Thukela

Nduze

Mvoti

Stanger/KwaDukuza

Wartburg

R614

Umhlali

Tongaat

Tongaat

Inanda
Dam

Umgeni

Pinetown

N
3

Durban

Durban International
Airport

R103

Park Rynie

0   10   20   30   40   50 km

Inset

N
3

Satya
Vardhak Sabha
Crematorium

OLD GREYTOWN

NEW GREYTOWN

OHRTMANN

LARCH MANNING

World's
View

OLD HOWICK RD   HOWICK

Natal
Botanical
Gardens

Bellewan

VICTORIA

BERG

PIETERMARITZ

LONGMARKET

LOOP

EAST

BOSHOFF

Sobantu

ZWARTKOP

MAYOR'S WALK

WEST

PINE

St George's
Garrison Church

Fort Napier

COLLEGE

DURBAN

ORIBI

Epworth

Italian Prisoner
of War Church

EDENDALE

Umsinduzi Canal

RICHMOND

RITCHIE

WASHINGTON

MARKET

N
3

C B DOWNES

MURRAY

0   1   2   3   4   5 km

Outlying areas

Fort Napier

After the British annexation of Natal in May 1843, an armed force consisting of two companies of the 45th Regiment established themselves strategically on a hill to the west of Pietermaritzburg. The next day, they started to build a primitive fort consisting of a central square with two flanking redoubts. The post was named Fort Napier after Sir George Napier, then governor of the Cape Colony. Within two years, the garrison had permanent buildings of stone and brick with tiled roofs. By the 1850s, there were approximately 550 men in the garrison, of which more than 400 were established at the fort.

It appears the fort's design was repeatedly modified as circumstances dictated. Barracks and a large number of buildings were added over time, undoubtedly to accommodate the large numbers of troops during the Anglo-Zulu War of 1878–79 and the first and second Anglo-Boer Wars. In 1876, a trench approximately three metres deep, with adjacent earthwork walls, was constructed around the fort. Stone walls, guns placed at various points and drawbridges to protect the main roadways, further improved the fort's defensibility.

Fort Napier was one of the most important military bases in South Africa. It played a major role in the military history of KwaZulu-Natal and in the economic and social development of Pietermaritzburg. The last garrison at Fort Napier was the South Staffordshire Regiment, which left on 14 August 1914. Between 1914 and 1918, Fort Napier served as an internment camp for German prisoners of war.

Fort Napier was once one of the most important military bases in South Africa.

The first veterinary laboratory

Embryo transplantation, a common veterinary procedure these days, was one of the many innovative and exciting projects undertaken at the State Veterinary Laboratory at Allerton, a suburb of Pietermaritzburg. The laboratory was built in 1897, mainly for veterinary research, and was the first of its kind in the country. Its founder, Dr Herbert Watkins-Pitchford, took up his post three days after his 30th birthday.

In the first 17 years of its existence, the laboratory played a key role in controlling contagious diseases, among them smallpox, glanders, wire worm and blue tongue in sheep. Vaccines were produced and water, food and drug analyses carried out. Diseases such as rabies and rinderpest (which was successfully stemmed before it could take a hold in the Colony) were also studied. For a long time, this was the only institution in South Africa where cancer could be diagnosed.

The State Veterinary Laboratory was used for research until 1928, when a new building was constructed for this purpose. From the 1950s onwards, it was used as offices for the regional director and state veterinary services. The typically Pietermaritzburg red-brick double-storey building is one of the few industrial buildings left from the previous century. It housed one of the first weather stations in the area, which was situated in the attic and protruded from the corrugated-iron roof.

The first bridge: Mooi River

Helen Bridge, across the Mooi River, was the first bridge built north of Pietermaritzburg. By 1886, there was a serious need for a bridge across the river because wet weather often delayed transport wagons. During flood, wagons, oxen, mules and servants had to camp on the banks of the river, waiting for a safe crossing. When the bridge was finally built at the crossing point, it played a significant role in the further development of the area.

Today, all that remains of the fort's original structure is a brick water tower constructed at the beginning of the 20th century on one of the old shale bastions. Among the later constructions that still stand are a recreation hall dating from around 1890, which was built in the verandah style typical of the time. Most of the woodwork on the porch is original, and rising above the roof is a clock tower with a deep well for weights. The officers' mess, which was used by the commandant of the prisoner of war camp at Fort Napier, is one of the finest wood-and-iron structures in South Africa. After World War I, it was rented out to various bodies until it finally became the library and occupational therapy centre for the Fort Napier Psychiatric Hospital in the late 1920s. Together with St George's Garrison Church, these buildings are among the most important reminders of British military presence in the country.

St George's Garrison Church

St George's Garrison Church was built at the request of Bishop Hamilton who, on being appointed to the diocese of Natal, was distressed to find that troops at Fort Napier had no church of their own in which to worship. In time, St George's Garrison Church became a memorial to British soldiers who had fallen in the wars against the Boers, Zulu and Matabele. The foundation stone of the church, which is part of Fort Napier, was laid in 1893 on land donated by the British War Office.

The stained-glass windows of the church were donated as a memorial to the British soldiers who fought in defence of the Colony. During the South African War of 1899–1902, St George's Garrison Church was used as a hospital. More than 400 soldiers were nursed there.

Over the years, many famous people, including Lord Baden-Powell, have visited St George's Garrison Church. Major-General Dan Pienaar, a World War II hero who had been incarcerated with his mother in a Pietermaritzburg concentration camp, came close to having a wounded leg amputated at the church in the days when it was being used as a military hospital.

Sobantu

Many of the original cottages in the village of Sobantu are still standing. They were built in 1924 after the Pietermaritzburg City Council, which had until then been unsure as to how to provide accommodation for black urban workers, decided to create a 'native village'. After some dispute, the village was established south of Bishopstowe Road, just outside Pietermaritzburg. The first houses were completed in 1928.

The new settlement was named Sobantu, which was the Zulu name of William Colenso, first Bishop of Natal, who had established his home and a mission station at Bishopstowe, near where Sobantu was eventually built. The name means 'father of the people' and is a mark of the respect and affection in which Bishop Colenso was held by the Zulu people.

Although initially there was resistance to the move, by 1930 many of Pietermaritzburg's married black workers had been moved into supervised accommodation in the village. In 1956, the government decided to relocate Sobantu, but the move never took place. Despite increasing tensions, Sobantu was considered a model village and it came as a shock to Pietermaritzburg's white residents when, in August 1959, riots broke out there.

Until 1960, Sobantu was the only official black residential area within the borough of Pietermaritzburg under direct control of the city council. Despite threats of removal for many years and the transfer of control from one administrative board to another, the village (now a sprawling township) remained at its original location.

An imperial garden

The Natal Botanical Gardens were founded in 1874 on a hillside that leads down to the ancient flood plain where the Dorpspruit joins the Umsinduzi River. Collecting and displaying indigenous African flora, particularly from East Africa, is now the main focus in the 49-hectare gardens. The past is evident in the large number of northern-hemisphere plants, especially the elegant avenue of London plane trees laid out in 1906.

In colonial times, the institution was particularly successful in raising exotic seedling timber and fruit trees for distribution, free or at a nominal charge. By 1880, five kinds of eucalyptus, five kinds of pine, three kinds of cypress and two types of acacia – including Black Wattle, which is now viewed as an invasive alien plant – were on offer to plantation owners. At the time, the famous Kew Garden in London considered the Natal Botanical Gardens to be 'the finest seedling-producing institution in the British Empire'.

Nature lovers will delight in the botanical gardens' rich plant life, which has been specially cultivated to attract birds, of which there are more than 150 recorded species. A replica of a traditional Zulu hut (below) is surrounded by a variety of medicinal indigenous plants.

Italian Prisoner of War Church

During World War II, 5 000 Italian and 3 000 German prisoners of war were held at a camp in Epworth, outside of Pietermaritzburg. In 1943, at the instigation of Father Giacolo Conte, the Italian prisoners began to build a small church within the camp boundaries. The church was consecrated on 19 March 1944 by the Apostolic Delegate to South Africa and dedicated to the Virgin of Graces to 'remind future generations of the suffering, passion and grief' of the Italian soldiers.

With great ingenuity and determination, the Italian prisoners blasted and cut stone from a quarry two kilometres away before transporting it, on foot, to the site of the church. Local builders, who were not familiar with the use of block stones for construction, 'passed from wonder to surprise in discovering its virtues'. The beams of the church are supported by 18 pillars, with a belfry rising ten metres on the left-hand side of the church.

In 1944, W G Lowe, the commandant at the prisoner of war camp, wrote in a small publication, *Prigionieri di Guerra Italiana: Campo di Pietermaritzburg*:

'The Church provides a long-felt want in the Camp, and the men obtain spiritual guidance and comfort from the ministrations of Padre Conte. I never hear the quiet tolling of the bell at

The Italian Prisoner of War Church outside Pietermaritzburg is a testament to the fine craftsmanship and skill of Italian prisoners of war in South Africa.

Howick Falls is one of the few natural sites in South Africa to be declared a national monument.

sunset or early in the morning, without thinking how grateful they must be for this link with their homes, many thousands of miles away.'

After the war, the church slowly fell into disrepair. It was restored in 1961 and reconsecrated the following year. Later, it was successfully repaired after being struck by lightning on the evening of 26 December 1985. Services are held there on the last Sunday of every month at 10h00. The church bell was a gift in 1963 from the MOTHS (Memorable Order of the Tin Hats) of Mentevelluna, the birthplace of the then Italian Consul, Dr A Benedetti.

In and around the Midlands

At much the same time as settlement of the southern coastal region began, the area to the northwest of Pietermaritzburg was being explored. The Voortrekkers were followed by British and other settlers, as well as missionaries of various denominations. The brothers from Mariannhill Monastery established many beautiful farms and schools on their mission stations, and had a substantial influence on the development of the KwaZulu-Natal Midlands.

Howick Falls

Howick Falls was declared a national monument in the 1950s. Known also as kwaNogqaza, 'the place of the tall one', the 100-metre-high falls are situated almost in the centre of the small town of Howick. The site of the waterfall is near the place where early settlers used to cross the Umgeni River, a dangerous passage, especially when the river was in flood. A bridge was built upstream and was moved in 1850 to within 200 metres of the edge of the falls in order to make the route into town more direct. There is now a safe viewing platform above the falls and a hiking trail down to the pools below.

KZN's oldest masonic lodge

The Carnarvon Lodge of Freemasons is the oldest country lodge in KwaZulu-Natal. It came into being on 31 October 1876, having received permission to use the name and coat of arms of the Earl of Carnarvon, then the Pro-Grand Master of English Freemasonry. The brethren of Carnavon bought two properties for the lodge, one of approximately eight hectares bordering the Illovo River not far from Richmond and the other in Russell Street in Richmond, where the temple was finally built in May 1883. The new temple was a simple rectangular structure with Victorian embellishments, measuring about nine by sixteen metres, with brick walls nearly four metres high.

Nelson Mandela's capture at Howick

On 5 August 1962, the South African Police arrested Nelson Mandela in Howick on a tip-off from an informer. By then, Mandela, later to become South Africa's first black president, had been operating underground for approximately 18 months.

In November 1962, Mandela was sentenced to five years' imprisonment for incitement to strike and for leaving the country without a passport. He was held for six months in Pretoria Prison before being transferred to Robben Island off Cape Town.

In 1963, while Mandela was still serving his sentence, he was called to stand trial with several fellow leaders of the African National Congress, who had been arrested on charges of plotting to overthrow the government. On 12 June 1964, eight of the accused, including Mandela, were sentenced to life imprisonment.

A memorial plaque in Howick marks the site of Mandela's capture.

Richmond and Byrne District Museum

Richmond was founded in 1850 by the Byrne settlers, who had started to arrive in the area in the mid-1800s as part of a settlement programme started by Reverend Joseph Byrne. Many of them were Presbyterian and of Scottish extraction.

The Richmond and Byrne District Museum building was built in 1882 as the manse for the congregation's first full-time minister, Reverend W D Barrie. It remained the property of the Church of Scotland and was used as a manse until Richmond's town board bought it in its centenary year. The building is typical of the period in plan and form, although unusual in that it is constructed out of shale, a material more often used by the Voortrekkers than by British settlers, except in the construction of churches.

The museum houses the Byrne Collection,

The Richmond and Byrne District Museum houses the Byrne Collection of furniture and other items made by early settlers to replace their lost possessions.

with carvings and furniture handcrafted from indigenous wood, testimony to the ingenuity of the settlers, who had lost all their possessions when one of their ships, the *Minerva*, sank in a storm on arrival at Durban. The museum also depicts the lives of the amaBhaca people who fled from repeated Zulu raids in the time of

Shaka, and those of the early Indian traders in the district.

Other important buildings in Richmond include the agricultural hall (where those involved in the Bhambata uprising of 1906 were tried) and St Mary's Anglican Church, which is one of the few buildings in KwaZulu-Natal designed by the famous architect Herbert Baker.

Fort Nottingham

Fort Nottingham was built in 1856 to protect both Boer and British settlers from cattle raids by Bushmen who were still living in the foothills of the Drakensberg mountains at the time. A small detachment of members of the 45th Regiment, together with the Cape Mounted Police, was stationed at the semicircular outpost of Fort Nottingham. Fort Nottingham was also an important base during the Langalibalele rebellion of 1873.

Richenau Mission

The first splinter mission of the Mariannhill Monastery near Pinetown was founded on the Polela River, near Underberg, in 1886. It was established at the request of the local chief, Sakayena, who wanted his people to learn 'the book' (the Christian Bible). The mission station was named Richenau after a Benedictine Abbey founded on the Isle of Lake Constance in Germany in AD 800.

Richenau Mission was the first 'satellite' mission established by brothers from the famous Mariannhill Monastery outside Durban.

The mission originally consisted of a wood-and-iron house that was erected around 1892. The mission church, with its yellowwood beams and fittings and walls hand-painted in German style, was built from local stone in 1898. The brothers at the Mariannhill Monastery made most of the stained-glass windows, although some were imported from the Tyrol, in Austria. From the choir stall, you can see the old belfry with three Austrian bells named St Mary, St Joseph and St Bernard.

A water mill near the waterfall on the nearby Polela River once provided hydroelectric power and, before that, turned the wheels of the mission's grain mill. The water wheel was still working in the late 1970s but has since been washed away by a flood. Apart from the mill, the mission had a bakery and blacksmith's forge, both now derelict, and a farm, which is now leased to a neighbouring farmer.

Centocow Mission, with its wonderful old buildings, continues to play a pivotal role in the social and spiritual life of the people in the Creighton area.

A small sign on the R617 near Underberg marks the turn-off to the mission, which is reached by way of an iron-and-stone bridge built by the Benedictine brothers more than a hundred years ago.

Centocow and Kevelaer Missions

The Centocow Mission was established in 1888 in the Creighton area, as was the impressive Kevelaer Mission near Donnybrook, founded by the inimitable Abbot Pfanner of the Mariannhill Monastery. Kevelaer was originally a halfway house to larger stations. It was officially declared a place of pilgrimage in 1953. The name comes from a famous place of pilgrimage in northern Germany. The mission became known for a famous painting, 'Our Lady, Consoler of the Afflicted', which still draws visitors to the beautifully restored church.

No longer under the jurisdiction of the Congregation of the Mariannhill Missions (CMM), the Centocow Mission continues to thrive under the direction of Polish priests. It has two magnificent red-brick churches, the smaller of which is no longer in use because of prohibitive maintenance and restoration costs. In its heyday, the mission housed 17 brothers and 100 labourers who worked in the beautiful orchards and vineyards. A convent of the Sisters of the Precious Blood was also part of the mission station.

The congregation at Centocow now comprises 8 000 to 10 000 people and the brothers serve 15 outstations. They are involved in a number of social projects to provide home-based care and to care for orphans.

The large hospital on the premises is not run by the mission.

Joseph Baynesfield gave Baynesfield Estate to the nation on very specific conditions.

Baynesfield Estate

The 24 000-hectare tract of land known as Baynesfield Estate, north of Richmond, was given to the nation as a gift by Joseph Baynes, with the proviso that the profits be used for agricultural development and research, education of black farmers, creation of a public park on the estate and the establishment of homes for both black and white children at Baynesfield. Baynes's house, the mausoleum that was constructed on the estate in 1923 after the death of his second wife,

the cattle dip and the dairy are all national monuments. Tours can be arranged through the beautifully restored Victorian manor-style house and the magnificent gardens. A small museum and an education centre are housed in the old dairy.

In his day, Joseph Baynes made an outstanding contribution to the development of agriculture in South Africa. He helped to introduce scientific farming methods in commercial agriculture. His large-scale commercial dairy farm thrived thanks to his use of electricity and mechanisation as well as advanced pasteurisation and refrigeration methods.

In the late 1890s, after his herds and those of other farmers were wiped out by rinderpest, Baynes imported 500 head of cattle from Australia, only to have all the bulls and all but 60 of the cows die from pleuropneumonia and redwater. In 1902, within three months of discovering that many of these diseases are tick-borne, Baynes became the first South African farmer to build a dipping tank and to dip his cattle. By 1909, dipping had rescued him from huge potential losses during the East Coast Fever epidemic and had enabled him to more than compensate for earlier losses amounting to £10 000.

Hopewell's glacial remains

Three hundred million years ago, southern Africa was part of the Gondwana supercontinent and largely covered by an ice cap similar to that over Antarctica today. The ice cap lasted 40 to 60 million years, its great bulk gradually moving in a southwesterly direction, abrading and polishing the bedrock over which it migrated. Today, you can still see these glacial striations south of the Umgeni River. They are preserved on a hard sandstone and suggest that the ice mass flowed off a highland region into a sedimentary basin.

The Lynmouth Glacial Pavement on Hopewell Farm (below), along the Baynesfield–Eston road south of Pietermaritzburg, is thought to be about 330 million years old. These unspoilt glacial striations were actually formed not by ice but by massive glacial debris, a paste of sand and silt set into the ice, which abraded the ground underneath at enormous pressure. The best striations are about two kilometres southeast of the Lynmouth homestead on Hopewell Farm, where a stream cuts through an outcrop of Table Mountain sandstone.

KZN's World Heritage Sites

KwaZulu-Natal is flanked on east and west by two World Heritage Sites – by definition 'important' parts of the Earth that the United Nations Educational, Scientific and Cultural Organization (UNESCO) helps to protect by granting them this status. World-renowned Heritage Sites include Australia's Great Barrier Reef, Zimbabwe's Victoria Falls, the Grand Canyon in the United States and the Great Wall of China. While sites must satisfy selection criteria to be included in the list, provision for the protection, management and integrity of the site is also important.

The Greater St Lucia Wetland Park in the north-east of KwaZulu-Natal was declared a World Heritage Site in December 1999, the first of nine South African World Heritage Sites currently registered. The park lies within the area known as Maputaland, which contains another site – Border Cave – that has been proposed for World Heritage status.

The uKhahlamba-Drakensberg Park was made a World Heritage Site in November 2000. Of the more than 700 World Heritage Sites on Earth, it is one of only 23 (in 14 countries) that are of both natural and cultural importance.

Other World Heritage Sites of purely cultural importance in South Africa are Robben Island in the Western Cape; the Cradle of Humankind fossil hominid sites of Sterkfontein, Swartkrans, Kromdraai and environs in Gauteng, Limpopo and North-West; and Mapungubwe in Limpopo. The Vredefort Dome in North-West and the Free State and the Cape Floral Kingdom are World Heritage Sites of natural significance.

The Amphitheatre towers in the background at the uKhahlamba-Drakensberg Park, one of KwaZulu-Natal's two World Heritage Sites.

The Drakensberg: a place of wonder

The great Drakensberg escarpment was created millions of years ago in the fusing and fracturing of the Earth's crust before the supercontinent of Gondwana fragmented and Africa was split off from Antarctica and the Falkland Plateau. At this time, the continent was being twisted and tilted, westward then eastward, elevating the interior. Finally, with the cooling of floods of magma, thick layers of basalt were superimposed. Over the next 100 million years, erosion pushed the Drakensberg escarpment 100 kilometres inland.

The Drakensberg contains some of the most important archaeological sites in southern Africa, some of which date back to the Earlier, Middle and Later Stone Ages. It is thought that the mountains have provided humans with sustenance and shelter for a million years.

Later Stone Age people, ancestors of the Bushmen, inhabited the area at least 8 000 years ago. The Bushmen have left a legacy of rock paintings in the mountain caves and rock shelters that used to be their homes. Their numbers were small, probably never larger than about a thousand within the borders of the present-day uKhahlamba-Drakensberg Park, and their ecological footprint was very light.

For a long time it was thought that the Bushmen were extinct in the area and that the last members of this ancient people were seen in the late 1800s by a couple honeymooning in the Drakensberg. Recent research, however, has discovered a number of groups, known as the 'Secret San', who are descendants of the original

A large section of the Drakensberg has been protected for over a century.

Drakensberg Bushmen. It is thought that their ancestors were either absorbed into Bantu-speaking clans or moved away into areas of less conflict.

uKhahlamba-Drakensberg Park

In 1903, a section of the spectacular mountain range on the border between South Africa and the mountain kingdom of Lesotho range was proclaimed a protected area, probably to act as a reserve for the fast-disappearing herds of eland and other antelope species and to preserve the scenic value of the area. In 1905, the area was set aside as a 'demarcated forest' and, in 1907, was proclaimed a game reserve, which enabled game protection laws to be enforced. As a result of these measures, a large portion of the present-day

---

Legend of the serpent

The massive mountain range on KwaZulu-Natal's western flank has been known by a number of evocative names. The Voortrekkers called it Drakensberg, meaning 'dragon mountains' – for them, this was the legendary abode of dragons, where mists and clouds swirled like fiery breath and jagged ramparts were reminiscent of ridged backs. To the Zulu, it was the uKhahlamba, or 'barrier of spears', because the dramatic mountain storms thundering off the mountains echoed with the same noise that was made by Zulu warriors beating cattle-hide shields on their way to war.

In the Kamberg area, the local Hlubi people believe that Inkanyamba, a python-like creature with a mane down his back and the face of an antelope, lives on top of Mpendle mountain. They say he can be heard roaring from his eyrie during berg thunderstorms, and that traditional healers have the power to see him as he travels along the mountaintops. Ordinary humans, however, should not even look for him for fear of untimely death.

Legend has it that the Drakensberg Bushmen could control this ferocious creature, a belief that caused people from all over southern Africa to seek them out as rainmakers.

park has enjoyed protection for over a century and is in pristine condition.

In its present incarnation, uKhahlamba-Drakensberg Park is 300 kilometres long and covers 243 000 hectares. For ease of description, it is generally divided into three sections. The southern areas include Garden Castle State Forest, the Mzimkhulu Wilderness area, Cobham and Vergelegen Nature Reserves, Loteni, the Mkhomazi Wilderness area and Kamberg. The central region, which is possibly the most developed from a tourism perspective, includes Giant's Castle, Monk's Cowl, Cathedral Peak, the Mdedelelo and Mlanbonja wilderness areas and Champagne Castle. To the far north is the Royal Natal National Park, where one finds the spectacular Mont-Aux-Sources amphitheatre with its great waterfall crashing off the escarpment.

The legacy of rock paintings by early Bushman hunter-gatherers lent considerable weight to the uKhahlamba-Drakensberg Park's bid for World Heritage status. Indeed, there is not such a dense collection of well-preserved and diverse rock paintings anywhere else in Africa, especially in the area south of the Sahara. Recent studies have recorded 600 painting sites containing some 40 000 images in the uKhahlamba-Drakensberg Park.

The uKhahlamba-Drakensberg Park ranks as one of seven biodiversity hotspots in southern Africa. There are at least 2 153 plant species, 299 species of bird, 48 mammal species, 48 reptile species and 26 frog species in the area. Many of the

species are endemic, while some 119 are listed as threatened in the international Red Data Book. Since 1987, several new species have been identified in the region, but many still remain undiscovered. The area's invertebrate fauna are particularly poorly described, although studies have been conducted on several species such as earthworms, crane flies, butterflies, dragonflies, millipedes, centipedes and lacewings. As with mammals and flora, many of these insect species are endemic to the region.

Cathedral Peak

The Cathedral Peak region is one of the most developed areas in the park and is the location of Ezemvelo KZN Wildlife's newest camp, Didima. Here you can overnight in a cave (without paintings since it is prohibited to stay in one that is so adorned) before seeking one of the many accessible rock-art sites with the help of a guide. Sebaeni (or Poacher's) Cave is considered to be one of the greatest rock-art galleries and is relatively easy to access.

A rock-art centre at Didima has been established to give those who are unable to walk to the caves access to the rock paintings. The San Art Interpretative Centre at Didima provides a fascinating background into the art and culture of the Bushmen through static displays and audio-visual presentations featuring a reconstructed cave covered with accurate reproductions of rock art.

Battle Cave

Battle Cave at Injama, which is adorned with some 750 paintings, gets its name from a red monochrome depiction of a fight between two Bushman groups. It is also one of the few sites in the Drakensberg where lions are depicted. The cave is open to the public on condition that visitors are accompanied by a registered guide.

Game Pass Shelter

The Drakensberg Bushmen have long since disappeared from the Kamberg region, but their influence lives on in many of the cultural practices of the local people and, of course, in beautiful rock paintings like those in the famous Game Pass Shelter, high in the Kamberg Nature Reserve.

Many experts consider the panels of rock paintings at Kamberg to be the 'Rosetta Stone' of

The Drakensberg is often surrounded in cloud, adding to the mystery of the area.

The art

The Drakensberg rock paintings are distinctive for their use of the shaded polychrome technique, in which human figures, eland and other animals are represented by using two colours – usually red and white – that delicately grade into each other. The minute detail contained in the paintings has also impressed researchers. Compared to rock art in other parts of the world, the Drakensberg images are small and intricate. An eland, for example, will be represented as a 35-centimetre-tall image with clearly indicated eyes, mouth and ears. It will have a mane of individually painted hairs no more than 1.5 millimetres long and neat black cloven hooves. Animals are shown not only side-on and walking or running, but also lying down, leaping, looking back over the shoulder – all in graded polychrome. Most remarkably, they are also viewed from the front and the rear. Human figures are also found in a range of sophisticated positions.

Academics differ on the interpretation of the images. Some appear to be direct illustrations from life, depicting, for example, mounted soldiers and sailing ships. Others appear to be symbolic, depicting the mystical rain dance or the spiritual value of the eland. The paintings are the only record we have of the culture and spiritual life of Bushman communities.

At the centre of Bushman spiritual belief is the concept of a spirit world that can be reached by people who possessed multifaceted supernatural powers. These people, the shamans, entered a state of trance at a communal trance dance or on their own. In this state, it was believed, they could cure the sick, make rain, guide antelope towards hunters and visit the spirit world to commune with their Creator and all the animals, especially the one most frequently painted, the eland. Nearly every shelter with rock art has at least one eland painting. Some have more than a hundred, many painted one on top of another.

A life-sized Bushmen display in memory of the Drakensberg's early inhabitants can be seen at Main Cave.

ancient rock art, providing the key to understanding the spiritual and ritual meanings of other Bushman art. They are also considered to be some of the finest examples of rock art in the country. If you are unable to make the fairly strenuous walk up to the shelter, there is also a San Rock Art Centre at Kamberg that shows an evocative video of paintings in the cave.

Unlike many archaeological sites worldwide that can be experienced only at a distance, at Kamberg you can climb right up to the Game Pass Shelter to view the paintings exactly where they were painted hundreds of years ago. One of the most intriguing panels depicts an eland in its death throes. Near the eland are anthropomorphic figures with antelope hooves instead of feet, symbolic of a shaman's state of trance.

It is not just the rock art that is ancient in Kamberg. The environment itself is a product of geomorphic processes that began millions of years ago and continue to this day. Down in the Kamberg valley, small rock shelters dating back 220 million years are embedded with tiny sparkles of quartz crystals. Layers of sedimentary sandstone contain the fossilised remains of ancient creatures that disappeared from the Earth some 250 million years ago during what is thought to be the greatest mass extinction ever, when 90 percent of all known species died out.

Main Cave at Giant's Castle

There were fewer than 30 eland in the Giant's Castle region in 1903, when an area of 12 140 hectares was set aside for them to roam freely. In 1947, the Natal Parks Board took control of the reserve and established the old Giant's Castle Camp on a grassy plain overlooking the Bushman's River. With subsequent additions, the reserve now stretches from Giant's Castle in the south to Injasuthi in the north – some 35 000 hectares of the 230-hectare uKhahlamba-Drakensberg Park.

Within easy walking distance of Giant's Castle Camp is an enormous overhang adorned with stunning rock art in an area that was last thought to be inhabited by the Bushmen before 1880. The overhang has been converted into a natural museum, Main Cave, where there is also a life-sized display of Bushmen.

Not far from the caves is a giant rock carved with a '75'. This marks the base camp established by Major Anthony Durnford when he led a military mission to close the entrances to some of the passes in the area to prevent further gun-running by the Basotho and the Hlubi. It is thought that the cook of the 75th Regiment of the Royal Engineers actually carved the number.

Main Cave can be visited in the company of a registered guide.

The Langalibalele rebellion

Langalibalele (meaning 'the sun is boiling hot') was the leader of the amaHlubi clan in the 1800s, at the time when the colonial government settled the clan on the banks of the Bushman's River to act as a buffer between the raiding Bushmen and the white settlers.

Many amaHlubi men had acquired firearms while working on the diamond fields of Lesotho. When the colonial government insisted they register the firearms, Langalibalele refused. Declared an outlaw, he retreated with his people up the Bushman's River valley through Giant's Castle, with Major Anthony Durnford and a unit of the Natal Carbineers in pursuit. Durnford and his men were attacked by amaHlubi warriors at the top of Bushman's Pass (now Langalibalele Pass). A stone cairn and aluminium cross mark the graves of the three Carbineers and two Zulu scouts who were killed at the top of the Pass before the unit fled. The Carbineers later exacted a savage revenge against the amaHlubi, killing at least 150 men, women and children and driving the clan away from the slopes of the Drakensberg.

Langalibalele escaped into the mountains of Lesotho, but was captured with his five sons and brought back in chains to a farcical trial in which he was banished to Robben Island, making him the first South African imprisoned there. He was eventually released. He died in 1889 and was buried in a secret cave in the shadow of Giant's Castle. Sixty-one years later, his grandson revealed the location of the cave. Nelson Mandela, Robben Island's most famous prisoner, flew by helicopter to lay a wreath at the site.

Cannibal Caves

Paintings in Cannibal Caves (southern Drakensberg) are faint and not nearly as interesting as the story behind the name: in the early 19th century, the caves used to be inhabited by a group of cannibals who, fleeing Shaka Zulu's reign of terror in the central part of the province, apparently found themselves without sources of food and had to turn to eating human flesh to survive.

Visit the rock-art sites

Rock-art sites in the area of the uKhahlamba-Drakensberg Park may be visited only in the company of a guide or park custodian. The guides are mostly Zulu speakers from nearby villages and have been trained to give tourists an insight into the symbolism of the rock paintings, as well as the natural environment through which visitors must walk in order to reach the sites. Many of the grasses and wild flowers along the way, for example, are still used by traditional healers relying on indigenous knowledge that has almost certainly been handed down from early Drakensberg Bushman inhabitants.

Maputaland: a well-kept secret

Maputaland runs from the St Lucia wetlands in the south to the Mozambican border in the north and from the Indian Ocean in the east to the Lebombo mountains in the west. Marketed as 'the Elephant Coast' (one of South Africa's best-kept tourism secrets), the area has a diverse range of ecosystems and a rich history of settlement.

The Thonga people of Maputaland have lived around Kosi Bay for at least 700 years and are excellent fishermen, using wooden fish traps or kraals to catch the fish on which they, largely, survive. The fish traps on Kosi Lake, which are thought to have originated around AD 1300, still feed communities living in this area and have been declared heritage sites of living history. It is possible for visitors to see the traps up close from a boat.

Traditional communities living in and around the Greater St Lucia Wetland Park have a long historical relationship with the land and natural environment. Indeed, this is one of the largest protected areas of recorded and potential Stone and Iron Age sites in the country. Traditional cultural and land-use practices continue to shape the present-day environment.

Greater St Lucia Wetland Park

The Greater St Lucia Wetland Park was formed in November 2000, consolidating 16 separately proclaimed areas into a single protected area. The park extends 230 kilometres from Mapelane, south of St Lucia to the Mozambique border. Its eastern boundary extends five kilometres out to sea, running parallel to the coast for the entire length of the park and encompasses the St Lucia Marine Protected Area. The western boundary is convoluted and runs from 1 to 54 kilometres west from the coast.

The area is cherished for its biodiversity, the result of the complex interplay between wetlands, estuaries, rivers, forested dunes and marine environments that include sea-turtle breeding beaches, coral reefs and submarine canyons inhabited by coelacanths.

Five distinct ecosystems coexist in the park, making it a habitat of critical importance for a long list of species from Africa's marine, wetland and savannah environments.

▶ The lake ecosystem consists of two lakes – Lake St Lucia and Kosi Lake – linked by estuaries and four large freshwater lakes. Lake St Lucia is the largest estuarine system in Africa and has several bird-rich islands.

▶ The marine ecosystem is characterised by long, sandy beaches and the warm waters of the Indian Ocean. The southernmost extension of coral reefs in Africa occurs here, as well as magnificent submarine canyons. Marine life includes

Kosi Bay: fish traps and palm wine

Kosi Bay is not a bay at all but rather an estuary consisting of four beautiful freshwater lakes that are strung like a delicate necklace for 18 kilometres before opening into the sea. It teems with fish, birds, crocodiles and hippopotami.

The traditional wooden fish traps of Thonga fishermen (bottom right) are carefully positioned close to the mouth of Makhawulani, Kosi's first lake, so that the larger fish are guided into the circular kraal, where they are ensnared, while the smaller fish can easily escape through the gaps between the wooden poles, ensuring a supply for later. The fishermen regularly wade out at low tide to check their traps, clearing them either by catching the fish by hand or spearing them.

When the apartheid government declared Kosi Bay a nature reserve and tried to forcibly remove three communities – the eKovokheni, the KwaDapha and the eMalangeni – from the area, the communities resisted in an ingenious way. With the help of David Webster, an anthropologist working in the area, they joined forces to establish a small tourist camp where visitors could visit local families, join them for a traditional meal, drink wine made from the Ilala Palm (bottom left) and listen to stories. The idea was that, if the camp was successful in attracting tourists, the people were less likely to be moved. The camp was indeed a success, and its inhabitants still clear the fish traps to feed their families.

Tragically, David Webster was not so lucky: he was murdered in his Johannesburg home by an apartheid hit squad in the 1980s.

Unlike the palms at Mtunzini, where the Raffia Palm Monument is situated, Kosi Bay's massive stands of Raffia Palms are a natural occurrence.

two threatened species of nesting sea turtles, the leatherback and the loggerhead, as well as whales, dolphins and whale sharks.

▶ The coastal dune system consists of linear dunes up to 180 metres high, sub-tropical forests, grassy plains and wetlands. Forested dunes separate Lake St Lucia from the sea.

▶ The Mkhuze and Mfolozi swamps, formed by washed-down river sediments, support swamp forests and extensive reed beds.

▶ The inland Western Shores have ancient shoreline terraces, fossilised marine life, sand forests and dry savannah vegetation.

The park is home to 48 threatened species and 147 that are on the international endangered species list. There are also 521 listed bird species, many of them endangered, and large breeding colonies of waterfowl. Among the larger inhabitants are various antelope species, giraffe, black rhino, elephant (recently reintroduced), buffalo, hippopotami and Nile crocodiles.

The park also contains four Ramsar sites, which are wetland sites of international importance. These are the St Lucia System, the turtle beaches and coral reefs of Tongaland, Lake Sibaya and the Kosi System.

Sir David Bruce Memorial Site

In 1887, Dr David Bruce discovered the causative agent of brucellosis, a serious cattle disease. He was subsequently sent to Natal to investigate a devastating, often fatal, livestock disease known as *nagana* that was rife in the colony and was causing farmers much hardship. Dr Bruce settled in the tiny northern village of Ubombo, fairly close to the present-day borders with Swaziland and Mozambique. The discoveries he made in that small village opened up new fields in both human and veterinary medicine.

Dr Bruce's study of the disease for two months in 1894–95 showed a strong connection with the tsetse fly. He later returned to Ubombo for two years to continue studying the disease. In 1903, he was sent to Uganda to investigate an outbreak of sleeping sickness. He found that the organisms in the cerebrospinal fluid of patients were the same as those transmitted to cattle by the tsetse fly. The discovery laid the foundation for the study of tsetse fly-transmitted trypansomiasis – the causative agent of both *nagana* and sleeping sickness in Africa.

The remains of Dr Bruce's camp have been found on the slopes of the Ubombo plateau.

Catalina Bay ruins

Catalina Bay on Lake St Lucia is named after the Royal Air Force's twin-engined Catalina seaplanes, which operated from there from 1942 to 1944 during World War II.

The Royal Air Force started sending Catalina squadrons on anti-submarine operations off the Cape, where German U-boats were operating in the early 1940s. As the U-boats moved eastwards the Catalinas followed, initially establishing a base at Congella in Durban harbour.

The first Catalinas arrived on the eastern shores of Lake St Lucia in December 1942. The Royal Air Force blasted the shore at Mission Rocks for concrete (the markings are still visible today) and built strip roads to the various installations along the dunes. The main base was on the eastern shores, site of the present-day private-tour launch jetty.

The Catalinas ran anti-submarine patrols from St Lucia all the way to Madagascar and down to Durban. Some of the German U-boat skippers fought back from the surface. More than once a Catalina would limp back to Catalina Bay, damaged by shells and trailing smoke. Two Catalinas actually went down into the lake in June 1943. The wreckage of one is still visible, while the other crashed near Charters Creek and has since disappeared.

Ruins associated with the Catalinas, such as a big slipway leading to a concrete apron, which was probably used to haul the Catalinas out for maintenance, can still be seen on the eastern shores. The last Catalina flew off St Lucia on 13 October 1944.

Border Cave

Border Cave was first investigated by Professor Raymond Dart during the 1930s. Excavations during the following half-century yielded a number of outstanding archaeological discoveries that have placed Border Cave among the most significant archaeological sites in Africa and the world. The cave takes its name from its location on the border of South Africa and Swaziland, with magnificent cliff-top views dropping 500 metres into the Swazi kingdom.

Humans have lived in Border Cave over an estimated period of 200 000 years. The human skeletal remains found in the cave are believed to be some of the oldest evidence of anatomically modern human beings. Various radiometric-dating techniques suggest that Middle Stone Age people were living at Border Cave more than 110 000 years ago.

Border Cave also has an impressively long and continuous stratigraphic record. A stratigraphic record is obtained by digging vertically into the cave floor and studying the human artefacts found in the various layers of ground. Each layer represents a different geological era and, through radiocarbon dating of organic material found in each of them, archaeologists can date the relative ages of the artefacts up to 40 000 years. Other dating techniques successfully used in the cave include electron spin resonance and thermoluminescence.

More than a million stone artefacts have been excavated in the cave, with some of the stone tools dating back as far as 100 000 years. An enormous amount of animal material has also been recovered from the cave, giving an indication of the food preferences of the prehistoric inhabitants: bush pig, warthog, zebra and buffalo featured regularly on the menu.

In 1942, an infant's skeleton was recovered from the cave. The bones were stained red, prompting archaeologists to think that the small body might have been painted prior to burial. The child had been buried with a shell ornament, suggesting that the people who buried it were capable of abstract and symbolic thought, which, in turn, implies a fairly complex language system.

Visit Border Cave

Border Cave is open to the public and is accessible on foot with the help of a guide from the local Mngomezulu community. There is an interpretative centre with dioramas and models, and a self-catering overnight camp was opened nearby. Call KwaZulu-Natal Tourism on (031) 337 8099 for more information.

ACKNOWLEDGEMENTS

I would like to thank the many people who have assisted me in compiling this book. Thank you to Alan Jackson, the staff of Amafa, in particular Corinne Winson and Nhlanhla Mkulisi, the staff at the Cultural History Museum, Durban, the Natal Museum, the Voortrekker Museum, the Natal Archives and Port Shepstone Museum.

A special thank you to my dear friend Craig Daniels who lent me a computer and a home after I had been twice robbed. A big thank you to Lee Rossini-Richter who lent me office space, made me tea and listened to my gnashing of teeth during the final stages of writing. I would especially like to thank the editors and staff at David Philip, New Africa Books, in particular Jeanne Hromnik, who nursed this project through to publication.

Thank you. It is people like you who make the sometimes difficult task of writing worthwhile in the end.

Index of place-names

The main sites that appear in the text and on the maps are listed below in alphabetical order.
The page number is given for the main entry only.